A POCKET GUIDE TO

Writing in History

A POCKET GUIDE TO

Writing in History

NINTH EDITION

Mary Lynn Rampolla

Trinity Washington University

bedford/st.martin's
Macmillan Learning
Boston | New York

For Bedford/St. Martin's

Vice President, Editorial, Macmillan Learning Humanities:
  Edwin Hill
Program Director for History: Michael Rosenberg
Program Manager for History: Laura Arcari
History Marketing Manager: Melissa Rodriguez
Director of Content Development: Jane Knetzger
Developmental Editor: Tess Fletcher
Associate Content Project Manager: Matt Glazer
Senior Content Workflow Manager: Jennifer Wetzel
Production Assistant: Brianna Lester
Senior Media Producer: Michelle Camisa
Editorial Assistant: Mollie Chandler
Editorial Services: Lumina Datamatics, Inc.
Composition: Lumina Datamatics, Inc.
Director of Rights and Permissions: Hilary Newman
Senior Art Director: Anna Palchik
Text Design: Claire Seng-Niemoeller
Cover Design: John Callahan
Printing and Binding: Edwards Brothers Malloy, Inc.

Manufactured in the United States of America.

2   1   0   9   8   7
f   e   d   c   b   a

For information, write: Bedford/St. Martin's, 75 Arlington Street, Boston,
MA 02116

ISBN 978-1-319-11302-5

Acknowledgments

*Art acknowledgments and copyrights appear on the same page as the art
selections they cover.*

Preface

Many students, like Jane Austen's Catherine Morland, assume that history is "tiresome," something only to be read "as a duty." They are often surprised to find that the discipline of history is both exciting and intellectually demanding. History students, like students of anthropology, sociology, and the other social sciences, are engaged in the challenging process of understanding the ideas, beliefs, and behaviors of people whose world view is often strikingly different from their own. In order to do this effectively, they must at the same time master a variety of critical thinking skills, become familiar with historical methodologies and approaches, and learn the conventions of reading, writing, and conducting research in the discipline of history. *A Pocket Guide to Writing in History* is designed to provide practical, quick-reference guidance for students about the various skills they will need to succeed in any undergraduate history course.

Now in its ninth edition, *A Pocket Guide to Writing in History* covers a wide range of topics with just enough depth, making it compact enough to tuck into a backpack or pocket. This new edition maintains the most valuable and enduring features of the prior eight editions, providing thorough coverage of the conventions for writing in history—from analyzing an assignment and conducting research, to working with written and nonwritten sources, writing effective papers and exams, avoiding plagiarism, documenting sources, and editing for clarity and style. Handy Tips for Writers boxes throughout provide checklists of suggestions on topics such as "Avoiding Plagiarism" and "Testing Your Thesis." Useful samples appear throughout the guide, including effective and ineffective examples of student writing and an annotated sample research paper, to illustrate each step of the writing process. An abundance of documentation models based on *The Chicago Manual of Style*, 17th edition, shows students how to cite print, electronic, and nonwritten sources.

The ninth edition offers new guidance on the fundamental, time-tested skills of "doing history," while also reflecting current trends in historical pedagogy and providing up-to-date advice regarding the integral role of technology throughout the process of writing and researching in history.

- Chapter 2 provides a comprehensive new section on evaluating online news sources and identifying fake news.
- In response to requests from both students and instructors, Chapter 3 includes a new example illustrating how to analyze a visual source.
- Chapter 4 now includes a list of additional on-line grammar resources.
- The documentation models in Chapter 7 have been updated to conform to the newest (17th) edition of *The Chicago Manual of Style*. New models providing guidance for citing social media sources have also been added to this section.

In working on this edition, I profited from the advice and encouragement of my colleagues at Trinity Washington University, especially my colleagues in the history program. I owe special thanks to my students, who have offered feedback and suggestions and whose efforts to become better writers and historians have always inspired me. I would also like to thank the teachers and scholars who reviewed the eighth edition and offered helpful suggestions and feedback.

At Bedford/St. Martin's, I would like to thank Chuck Christensen and Joan Feinberg, who conceived the original idea for this book. Special thanks go to Michael Rosenberg, Publisher for History and my development editor, Tess Fletcher, whose careful reading and thoughtful suggestions have contributed so much to improving this edition. I would also like to thank Matt Glazer, Associate Content Project Manager, and copyeditor Chris Parent. I am particularly grateful to my husband, Martin, who has patiently supported my work on this book through many years and nine editions.

Mary Lynn Rampolla
Trinity Washington University

A POCKET GUIDE TO

Writing in History

1

Introduction

WHY STUDY HISTORY?

As any Harry Potter fan knows, the most boring class at Hogwarts School of Witchcraft and Wizardry is History of Magic, taught by the dead (and "deadly dull") Professor Binns. Asked on one occasion about an unsolved mystery involving the school's past, Binns replies, "My subject is History of Magic. . . . I deal with facts, Miss Granger, not myths and legends."[1] Students who take their first college history class with a sense of foreboding often think that real historians, like Professor Binns, are interested only in compiling lists of names, dates, places, and "important" events that happened sometime in the past. But history is much more than this. The historian's goal is not to collect "facts" about the past, but rather to acquire insight into the ideas and realities that shaped the lives of men and women of earlier societies. Some beliefs and institutions of the past may seem alien to us; others are all too familiar. But in either case, when we study the people of the past, what we are really learning about is the rich diversity of human experience. The study of history is the study of the beliefs and desires, the practices and institutions, of human beings.

Why should we bother studying the past in our increasingly future-oriented society? There are as many answers to that question as there are historians. First, a thoughtful examination of the past can tell us a great deal about how we came to be who we are. When we study history, we are looking at the roots of modern institutions, ideas, values, and problems. Second, the effort we put into grappling with the worldviews of earlier societies teaches us to see the world through different eyes. The ability to recognize the meaning of events from a perspective other than our own is of inestimable value in our increasingly complex and multicultural society. An understanding of how past

1. J. K. Rowling, *Harry Potter and the Chamber of Secrets* (New York: Scholastic Press, 1999), 148–49.

events have shaped the complex problems of our own times can help us make informed decisions about our future.

In addition to introducing you to some of the basic elements of what historians do, this manual provides guidelines for writing papers in the field of history at all levels, from first-year surveys to upper-division seminars. The vast majority of students enrolled in an undergraduate history course are not contemplating a career in history. Nevertheless, the skills you will need to write an effective history paper—reading critically, thinking analytically, arguing persuasively, writing clearly, and organizing ideas logically—will be useful to you wherever your academic interests take you and in whatever career path you choose to follow.

1a   Asking historical questions

Historians come to their work with a deep curiosity about the past; to satisfy that curiosity, they ask some of the same questions detectives and journalists ask: *Who? What? When? Where?* and *Why?* Some of those questions are designed to elicit "the facts" and are relatively easy to answer: *Who* was the emperor of Japan during World War II? *What* tools did eighteenth-century weavers use? *When* did the Vietnamese drive the Khmer Rouge out of Phnom Penh? *Where* was the first successful French settlement in Canada? Other questions, however, are less easy to answer: *Who* was Jack the Ripper? *What* were the religious beliefs of the peasants of twelfth-century Languedoc? *When* did President Nixon learn about the Watergate break-in? *Where* did the inhabitants of the original settlement at Roanoke go? *Why* did the civilization of the ancient Maya collapse? Complex questions such as these have formed the basis of absorbing historical studies.

For both professional historians and students, asking questions lies at the heart of historical thinking and inquiry. As you will see in subsequent chapters, most of the reading and writing assignments you will encounter in your history classes begin with a question, whether that question is originally posed by your professor or is one that you develop for yourself as you embark on a research paper of your own design (see 5a-2). In either case, the central role of asking questions demonstrates that history is not about memorizing "facts," but about interacting with and thinking about the past.

1b Developing historical thinking skills

Students most often encounter history for the first time in a textbook assigned for their class. As a result, they sometimes think that "learning history" involves passively absorbing the narrative that is presented there, while the documents they read—found in a sourcebook, online, or embedded in the textbook—merely provide examples that illustrate that narrative. The truth is exactly the opposite: history—whether you encounter it in a textbook, a monograph, or an article in a scholarly journal—grows out of the evidence that is found in primary source documents and artifacts. In other words, the evidence comes first, and it is the historian's job to evaluate and organize that evidence. (For more on primary sources, see Chapter 2.)

Historians employ a variety of critical thinking skills in order to understand the documents and artifacts that provide their primary source materials, use the evidence from those sources to develop their own interpretations of the past, and evaluate the arguments and interpretations of other historians. The following are the most important skills for thinking critically about history; you will meet them again, and explore them in more detail, in the chapters that follow.

Use of historical evidence. When evaluating historical evidence, you should always consider basic questions such as: Who created the document or artifact? Who was the intended audience, and for what purpose was the source made or written? For documents, note what kinds of adjectives the author uses to describe people, places, or events, and the kinds of analogies or metaphors he or she employs. Considering the use of language can help you uncover the author's biases, point of view, and unspoken assumptions. These topics, which are discussed in more detail in 2b-1, form the basis of all critical thinking about historical evidence.

As you work with your sources, you should also ask whether the evidence you are considering is actually relevant to your topic. For example, a fascinating book about the Salem witch trials would not be *relevant* to a paper on witchcraft in Europe during the Middle Ages. Consider also whether your evidence is *sufficient* to demonstrate your point. If you are using statistical evidence, for example, the sample size is important; you cannot make a generalization about the impact of climate change on wheat production during the Little Ice Age in Europe based on evidence provided from one town in France. Finally, you should consider what *inferences* or generalizations you can legitimately draw from the kind of evidence you are using. For example, while trials and court cases are very useful sources for historians, we cannot draw generalizations about how most people in a particular time or place behaved based on the alleged actions of a single person: the trial of a sixteenth-century Italian peasant for necromancy does not suggest that most peasants of the time practiced black magic. We can, however, draw some inferences about the values and beliefs of his society since, by definition, a trial occurs when someone is accused of transgressing social or cultural norms.

Comparison.   Historians almost never rely solely on the evidence provided by a single source. Comparing sources helps historians determine "what happened"; if several sources recount an event in the same way, we can feel a bit more confident in the story they tell, particularly if those accounts are written by people with differing backgrounds or viewpoints. Where sources disagree, we can often learn something about their authors' beliefs, biases, and viewpoints. Considering multiple perspectives on the same event can illuminate important issues of interest to historians, including gender roles, social and economic class differences, religious beliefs and cultural practices, and so forth. Historians also compare related events and developments within or between societies. The skill of comparison is so important to historical thinking that the comparative paper is one of the most frequently assigned essays in undergraduate classes (see 3c-2).

Contextualization.   An essential element in critical thinking about history is understanding the *context* in which events occurred. For instance, a historian interested in nineteenth-century science would not examine the publication of Charles Darwin's theory of evolution by means of natural selection in terms of its impact on science alone. Science takes place within a social and cultural context, and scientific ideas can have a deep impact on politics, religion, education, and a host of other social institutions. Therefore, a historian would also consider such contextual questions as: What role did political issues play in the acceptance or rejection of Darwin's theory? What contemporary theories about the natural world influenced Darwin? Why did some theologians find his ideas threatening to religion while others did not? What impact did larger social, political, and intellectual movements and institutions have on the study of biology in this period? In other words, historians do not examine events in isolation; rather, they try to understand the people and events of the past in terms of the unique historical context that helped shape them.

Causation.   Historians are also interested in issues of causation. The historical events that you will be studying and writing about can almost never be traced to a single cause, and historians are careful to avoid simplistic cause-and-effect relationships as explanations for events. For example, although the assassination of Archduke Franz Ferdinand is often cited as the event that precipitated World War I, no historian would argue that it *caused* the war. Rather, historians try to uncover the complex multiplicity of causes that grow out of the historical context in which events occurred.

In considering causation, make sure you don't confuse causation with correlation. Correlation simply means that two or more events happened at about the same time. For example, a fiery comet could be seen throughout Europe in 1066. Later that year, William of Normandy invaded and conquered England. These two events are correlated, but to say that the comet was the cause of the Norman Conquest would be a logical fallacy (for more on this issue, see 2b-2).

Continuity and Change over Time.   An issue of particular interest to historians is the relationship between *continuity* (things that remain the same over time) and *change*. For example, a historian evaluating the impact of the Black Death on the economic and legal status of European peasants would examine the changes brought about by the bubonic plague against the backdrop of the ongoing institution of serfdom. Similarly, a historian studying the emergence of the People's Republic of China would consider both the changes wrought by the Cultural

Revolution and the persistence of traditional practices and customs under the communist regime.

Interpretation.   The eminent historian E. H. Carr wrote, "The historian without his facts is rootless and futile; the facts without their historian are dead and meaningless."[2] That is to say, historical sources must be *interpreted*; it is up to the historian to determine what the sources can tell us. Recognizing that historians interpret primary sources is an important aspect of approaching secondary sources—books and articles written by historians—critically. (For more on secondary sources, see 2a-2 and 2b-2.)

Historians, like the people they study, are part of a larger context. They are guided in their choice of subject by their own interests, which are in turn influenced by the time and place in which they live. As they ask new questions, historians look at sources in new ways. For example, in the 1950s, many standard U.S. history textbooks described Christopher Columbus as a heroic explorer; modern historians, writing from a more global perspective, have focused attention on the impact Columbus's explorations had on the indigenous peoples of the Americas. Historians may even discover "new" sources—sources that had always existed but had been ignored or dismissed as irrelevant. For example, the civil rights movement helped draw historians' attention to the central role of minorities in U.S. history. Finally, historians develop their interpretations from a variety of recognized perspectives within their discipline: there are feminist historians, economic historians, social historians, and so forth. Understanding the perspective from which a historian approaches the past provides an essential critical perspective to your evaluation of his or her work.

Periodization.   Periodization—the organization of the past into segments that share similar characteristics—is an artificial construct of historians. It is useful to be able to talk about "Late Antiquity" or "the Progressive era," but, since history is concerned with both change and continuity, determining when a particular period started or ended must inevitably be somewhat arbitrary. In thinking about periodization, much depends on the particular kind of history you are considering (political, economic, social, and so forth) and which events are singled out as significant "turning points." In considering when the Middle Ages

2. E. H. Carr, *What Is History?* (London: Penguin Books, 1961), 30.

ended and the early modern period began, for example, different historians might point to the Black Death, the rise of humanism, the Reformation, the voyages of Columbus, or the Scientific Revolution as defining transitions.

Argumentation.   Once you realize that history is not about recording "facts," it is easy to see that writing about history is not a simple matter of describing "what happened." Rather, historians evaluate and interpret the evidence of their sources and then construct arguments supporting the conclusion they have reached about the meaning and significance of that evidence. As a history student, you will be concerned with the skill of argumentation in two ways. First, as you read secondary sources, you will need to critically evaluate the argument their authors make: What is the author's thesis? What evidence does he or she use to support that thesis? Is the argument logical, plausible, and persuasive? You can find advice on evaluating the arguments of secondary sources in 2b-2. In addition, in your writing assignments you will usually be required to construct an argument in support of a thesis, based on the evidence of your sources. For more detailed advice on crafting a historical argument, see 4d.

Synthesis.   Synthesis is the most complex and challenging critical thinking skill that you will need to master in your study of history, one that draws on all of the other historical thinking skills. Synthesis involves analyzing and evaluating multiple sources, examining their relationship to each other, and developing a new perspective on the topic you are exploring. Many history assignments, especially research papers, involve synthesis. To write a research paper, you need to identify sources that are relevant to your topic, evaluate the usefulness of those sources, and synthesize the information they contain. You will need to evaluate both primary and secondary sources that may offer conflicting information and points of view, and work with sources that are biased, imperfect, or ambiguous. Finally, you will need to develop a thesis that reflects the conclusion you have reached as a result of your examination of these disparate historical sources, and organize and present an argument in support of that thesis in a systematic and clear fashion. The challenge posed by critical thinking at this level is not insignificant but, in the end, you will have truly entered the historian's world by developing a new understanding of the past.

2
Working with Sources

As you begin to think about historical questions, you will find that your search for answers will require you to explore many different kinds of sources. You will look at materials written in the period you are studying, and you will read books and articles written by modern historians. You may examine maps, photographs, paintings, and pottery. Ultimately, you may discover that you need to broaden your knowledge in several allied fields, for history often takes its practitioners into all manner of related disciplines: literary criticism, art history, and archaeology; political science, economics, and sociology. In any case, you will need to learn how to work with the sources on which the study of history is based.

2a Identifying historical sources

To answer their questions, historians evaluate, organize, and interpret a wide variety of sources. These sources fall into two broad categories: primary sources and secondary sources. To study history and write history papers, you will need to know how to work with both kinds of sources.

2a-1 Primary sources

Primary sources are materials produced by people or groups directly involved in the event or topic under consideration, either as participants or as witnesses. These sources provide the evidence on which historians rely in order to describe and interpret the past. Some primary sources are written documents, such as letters; diaries; newspaper and magazine articles; speeches; autobiographies; treatises; census data; and marriage, birth, and death registers. In addition, historians often examine primary sources that are not written, like works of art, films, recordings, items of clothing, household objects, tools, and archaeological

remains. For recent history, oral sources, such as interviews with Iraq War veterans or Holocaust survivors and
other such eyewitness accounts, can also be primary
sources. By examining primary sources, historians gain
insights into the thoughts, behaviors, and experiences of
the people of the past.

Sometimes, you may be able to work directly with primary source materials, such as letters or manuscripts in
an archive. More often, you will use print or electronic
versions of sources, such as edited and/or translated
collections of letters or documents, images of maps or
paintings, or facsimiles. (For more on evaluating edited
and translated sources, see p. 16.) In either case, primary
sources provide windows into the past that allow you to
develop your own interpretation, rather than rely on the
interpretation of another historian.

Note: If you are using a collection of documents brought
together in a single volume, the preface, introduction,
headnotes to the documents, and other materials written by the editor or translator are considered secondary
sources; however, *the documents themselves*—letters, wills,
poems, sermons, and so on—are primary sources. (See 2a-2
for a discussion of secondary sources. For information on
how to cite the parts of an edited volume, see pp. 130–134.)

2a-2 Secondary sources

As a student of history, you will also use *secondary
sources*. Unlike primary sources, secondary sources are
texts—such as books, articles, or documentary films—
that are written or created by people who were not eyewitnesses to the events or period in question; instead,
the authors of secondary sources synthesize, analyze,
and interpret primary sources. Secondary sources may
be written by professional historians, but popular writers and journalists also write books and articles about
historical subjects. For an academic paper, you will usually want to consult scholarly works, not popular ones.
(For tips on how to distinguish popular from scholarly
sources, see pp. 20–21.)

Secondary sources are extremely useful. Reading secondary sources is often the simplest and quickest way to
become acquainted with what is already known about the
subject you are studying. In addition, examining scholarly books and articles will inform you about the ways

in which other historians have understood and interpreted events. Reading a variety of secondary sources is also the best way to become aware of the issues and interpretations that are the subject of controversy and debate among professional historians, debates in which you, as a student of history, are invited to participate. Moreover, the bibliographies of secondary sources can direct you to primary sources and additional secondary sources that you might find useful.

As valuable as secondary sources are, you should never base a history paper on them alone, unless, of course, you are writing a historiography paper (see 3d-2). Whenever possible, you should work from primary sources, studying the events of the past in the words of people who experienced, witnessed, or participated in them.

Note: As a student of history, you will also encounter *tertiary sources*, such as encyclopedias, dictionaries, and textbooks. Unlike secondary sources, which provide analysis and interpretation of primary sources, tertiary sources usually do not reflect new historical research; rather, they summarize and synthesize secondary sources. When you write an academic paper, it is not acceptable to rely on tertiary sources; most professors will not accept them as appropriate sources to cite in your bibliography. However, a textbook or an encyclopedia article can be a useful introduction to a subject that is new to you.

2a-3 Primary or secondary? The changing status of a source

While the definitions provided above seem fairly straightforward, it is not always easy to determine whether a particular text is a primary source or a secondary source. This is because the status of a source as primary or secondary does not depend on how old the source is, but rather on the historical question you are asking. For example, if you are writing about the reign of Julius Caesar (100–44 BCE), Suetonius's *Lives of the Twelve Caesars*, written in the early second century CE, would be a *secondary* source because Suetonius was not a witness to the events he describes. If, however, you are writing about the debates among second-century Romans about the use and abuse of imperial power, Suetonius's work would be a *primary* source. Thus, the status of a source as primary or secondary depends on the focus of your research.

2a-4 Accessing sources in history

Both primary and secondary sources often exist in multiple formats. Although the same source might be available in a printed book, on a website, or on microfilm, how you access a source does *not* affect its status as primary or secondary. Think about your university library: you can find both primary sources (such as collections of letters, newspapers, and photographs) and secondary sources (such as journal articles and books) in its print collection; some sources, such as newspapers and magazines, can also be found on microfilm. You can also find both primary and secondary sources online. For example, *The Complete Work of Charles Darwin Online*, published online by Cambridge University (http://darwin-online.org.uk), includes facsimiles of Darwin's notebooks, letters, and other original documents that would be considered primary sources. Similarly, you can find many secondary sources online. An increasing number of scholarly peer-reviewed journals are published solely in electronic formats; in addition, many academic articles that originally appeared in print journals can be accessed through electronic databases or archives such as *JSTOR*. (For more information about electronic databases, see 5c-5.) Whether you access such articles in print or online, these are secondary sources.

2a-5 Uses of primary and secondary sources

Both primary and secondary sources can provide valuable information; however, they provide different kinds of information. Primary sources allow you to enter the lives and minds of the people you are studying. The documents people wrote—sermons and wills, novels and poems—and the things they made—music and movies, knife blades and buttons—bring you into direct contact with the world of the past. Secondary sources provide a broader perspective on the events of the past and allow you to see them in context. Historians can present multiple points of view, have access to a wide range of documents, and are aware of the outcome of historical events, giving them a perspective that no single participant could have. In studying nineteenth-century communes, for example, primary sources such as diaries, letters, or items that commune members produced and used can provide firsthand information about the thoughts, feelings, and daily lives of the people who lived in such communities. Primary sources would be less useful, however, in examining the larger sociological effects of communal living. To get a better understanding of those effects, secondary sources in which historians examine several such communities over time, or study the ways in which contemporary outsiders viewed communes, might prove more useful. In your own work, you will need to use both primary and secondary sources, always keeping in mind what kinds of information each of those sources can give you about a topic.

2b   Evaluating sources

If primary sources always told the truth, the historian's job would be much easier—and also rather boring. But sources, like witnesses in a murder case, often lie. Sometimes they lie on purpose, telling untruths to further a specific ideological, philosophical, personal, or political agenda. Sometimes they lie by omission, leaving out bits of information that are crucial to interpreting an event. Sometimes sources mislead unintentionally because the authors' facts were incomplete, incorrect, or misinterpreted. Many sources are biased, either consciously or unconsciously, and contain unstated assumptions; all reflect the interests and concerns of their authors. Moreover, primary sources often conflict. As a result, one of the challenges historians face in writing about history is evaluating the reliability and usefulness of their sources.

Like primary sources, secondary sources may contradict one another. Several historians can examine the same set of materials and interpret them in very different ways. Similarly, historians can try to answer the same questions by looking at different kinds of evidence or by using different methods to gather, evaluate, and interpret evidence. To get the most out of your reading of secondary sources, you will need to study a variety of interpretations of historical events and issues.

You can find general advice about critical reading in Chapter 3 (see 3a); the following sections provide specific suggestions for evaluating both primary and secondary sources.

Tips for Writers
Questions for Evaluating Text-Based Primary Sources

- Who is the author?
- When was the source composed?
- Who was the intended audience?
- What is the purpose of the source? (Note that some primary sources, such as letters to the editor, have a central theme or argument and are intended to persuade; others, such as census data, are purely factual.)
- What is the historical context in which the source was written and read?
- How do the author's gender and socioeconomic class compare to those of the people about whom he or she is writing?
- What unspoken assumptions does the text contain?
- What biases are detectable in the source?
- Was the original text commissioned by anyone or published by a press with a particular viewpoint?
- How do other contemporary sources compare with this one?

Special considerations for editions and translations

- Is the source complete? If not, does the text contain an introductory note explaining editorial decisions?
- If you are using a document in a collection, does the editor explain his or her process of selection and/or translation?
- Are there notes introducing individual documents that provide useful information about the text?
- Are there footnotes or endnotes that alert you to alternate readings or translations of the material in the text?
- Does the edition or translation you are using most accurately reflect the current state of scholarship?

2b-1 Evaluating primary sources

Since primary sources originate in the actual period under discussion, we might be inclined to implicitly trust what they say. After all, if the author is an eyewitness, why should anyone doubt his or her word? Alternatively, we might lean toward dismissing primary sources altogether on the grounds that they are too subjective; as

Tips for Writers

Questions for Evaluating Nonwritten Primary Sources

For artifacts

- When and where was the artifact made?
- Who might have used it, and what might it have been used for?
- What does the artifact tell us about the people who made and used it and the period in which it was made?

For art works (paintings, sculpture, and so on)

- Who is the artist, and how does the work compare to his or her other works?
- When and why was the work made? Was it commissioned? If so, by whom?
- Was the work part of a larger artistic or intellectual movement?
- Where was the work first displayed? How did contemporaries respond to it? How do their responses compare to the ways in which it is understood now?

For photographs

- Who is the photographer? Why did he or she take this photograph?
- Where was the photograph first published or displayed? Did that publication or venue have a particular mission or point of view?
- Do any obvious details such as angle, contrast, or cropping suggest bias?

For cartoons

- What is the message of the cartoon? How do words and images combine to convey that message?
- In what kind of publication (for example, a newspaper or a magazine) did it originally appear? Did that publication have a particular agenda or mission?
- When did the cartoon appear? How might its historical context be significant?

For maps

- What kind of map is this (for example, topographical, political, or military)?
- Where and when was the map made? What was its intended purpose?
- Does the map contain any extraneous text or images? If so, what do they add to our understanding of the map itself?

For video and film

- What kind of film is this (for example, a documentary or a feature film)?
- Who are the director, the producer, and the screenwriter for the film? Have they made other films to which you can compare this one?
- Who is the intended audience? Why was the film made?
- Does the film use particular cinematic techniques that convey a particular mood or tone? (For more on analyzing film, see 3e.)

For sound recordings

- Who made the recording, and what kind of recording is it (music, speech, interview, and so on)?
- Was the recording originally intended for broadcast? If so, why was it broadcast, and who was the intended audience?

---

any police investigator could tell you, eyewitnesses see different things and remember them in different ways. In fact, historians steer a middle ground between these two approaches. Although primary sources comprise the basic material with which they work, historians do not take the evidence provided by such sources simply at face value. Like good detectives, they evaluate the evidence, approaching their sources analytically and critically.

Historians have developed a variety of techniques for evaluating primary sources. One such technique is to compare sources; a fact or description contained in one source is more likely to be accepted as trustworthy if other sources support or corroborate it. Another technique is to identify the authors' biases. For example, the historian Polydore Vergil asserted in his book *Anglica Historia* that King Richard III killed his nephews. Since Vergil was a contemporary of Richard III, you might accept his account at face value, unless you were also aware that the book was commissioned by King Henry VII, an enemy of Richard III who had organized a rebellion against him, killed him in battle, and seized his throne. Taking this fact into consideration, you would want to approach Vergil's work with a more critical eye, considering whether his loyalty to his employer led to any bias in his history. Historians also read their sources carefully for evidence of internal contradictions or logical inconsistencies, and they pay attention to their sources' use of language, since the adjectives and metaphors an author uses can point to hidden biases and unspoken assumptions.

Thinking about editions and translations.   As an undergraduate, you will probably not have the opportunity that professional historians do to work with original documents in their original languages. Instead, you will likely be relying on published, translated editions of primary sources or on documents found on the Internet.

Using modern editions of sources in translation is an excellent way to enter into the worldview of the people you are studying. Be aware, however, that any edited text reflects, to some extent, the interests and experiences of the editor or translator. For example, the process by which the editor of a document collection selects which documents to include and which to leave out involves interpretation: the collection, as it appears in print, reflects how the editor has understood and organized the material and what he or she sees as significant. Similarly, excerpts from a long document can be useful in introducing you to the basic content and flavor of the document, but it is important to note that in the process of choosing excerpts, the editor is making a judgment about what aspects of the source are important. You should read the whole source, if possible, rather than excerpts, in order to understand the significance of the entire document and the context of any portions of the source that you wish to discuss or quote. A scholar or an archivist developing a website is, of course, making similar choices about which primary sources to include, how and in what order they will appear on the web page, and how they will be edited and linked to one another and to other websites. Finally, translation always involves decisions about word choice and grammar that can range from inconsequential to very significant.

Note: Often, the introduction to an edited volume, the home page on a website, or the short headnotes that introduce individual texts in a print or online collection not only will provide useful background information about the text but also will alert you to the editor's choices and intentions.

To be effective research sources, primary documents require both careful and critical reading. When you analyze a primary source, keep in mind the questions in the Tips for Writers box on page 13.

Thinking about nonwritten primary sources. Although historians work mainly from written sources, they also use a
wide variety of nonwritten materials, including works of
art, photographs, maps, and audio and video recordings.
When dealing with nonwritten primary sources, you
should consider the same questions about author, audience, and context that are outlined in the Tips for Writers
box on page 13, while adding the questions from the Tips
for Writers box on pages 14–15 that are specific to the type
of source you are considering.

Evaluating primary sources: an example. In a letter written to
Sheikh El-Messiri in 1798, Napoleon expresses the hope
that the sheik will soon establish a government in Egypt
based on the principles of the Qur'an, the sacred text of
Islam. Those principles, according to Napoleon, "alone are
true and capable of bringing happiness to men."[1] Should
we assume, on the evidence of this letter, that Napoleon
believed in the truth of Islam? A historian might ask,
"Do we have any other evidence for Napoleon's attitude
toward Islam? What do other primary sources tell us about
Napoleon's attitude toward religions such as Catholicism,
Protestantism, and Judaism? Do any other primary sources
contradict the attitude toward Islam expressed in Napoleon's letter to the sheikh?" In other words, "How accurately and to what extent can this source answer questions
about Napoleon's religious beliefs?" In addition, historians try to understand or interpret their sources even if
those sources do not offer the best or most accurate information on a certain topic. As it happens, Napoleon did
not believe in Islam. This does not mean, however, that
his letter to the sheikh has no value. Instead, a good historian will ask, "Under what circumstances did Napoleon
write this letter? Who was Sheikh El-Messiri, and what was
his relationship to Napoleon? What does this letter tell us
about Napoleon's willingness to use religion to his political advantage?" Thus, to write about historical questions,
you will need to know how to approach many different
kinds of primary sources and ask appropriate questions
of them. (For more on writing about primary sources, see
Chapters 3 and 4.)

1. Napoleon Bonaparte, "Letter to the Sheik El-Messiri," in *The
Mind of Napoleon: A Selection from His Written and Spoken Words*, 4th
ed., trans. and ed. J. Christopher Herold (New York: Columbia University Press, 1969), 104.

2b-2 Evaluating secondary sources

Reading secondary sources helps us understand how other historians have interpreted the primary sources for the period being studied. Students sometimes hesitate to question the conclusions of established scholars; nevertheless, as with primary sources, it is important to read secondary sources critically and analytically, asking the same questions you ask of primary sources. Evaluate a secondary source by considering the points in this section and asking the critical questions listed in the Tips for Writers box below. (For more on critical reading, see 3a.)

Tips for Writers
Questions for Evaluating Secondary Sources

- Who is the author? What are his or her academic credentials? (You will often find information about the author in the preface of a book; journals sometimes include authors' biographies, either on the first page of the article or in a separate section.)
- When was the text written?
- What is the political, social, and cultural context in which the source was written?
- Who is the publisher? Is the text published by a scholarly press or a popular one? (For more information on scholarly and popular presses, see p. 20.)
- Who is the intended audience for the text (scholars, students, general reading public, or some other audience)?
- What is the author's main argument or thesis? (For more on identifying the author's thesis, see p. 28.)
- Does the author use primary sources as evidence to support his or her thesis? Is the author's interpretation of the primary sources persuasive?
- Are you aware of any primary source evidence that the author does not consider?
- Does the author contradict or disagree with others who have written on the subject? If so, does he or she acknowledge and effectively address opposing arguments or interpretations?
- Do the footnotes/endnotes and bibliography reference other important works on the same topic?
- Does the author build his or her argument on any unsubstantiated assumptions? (See pp. 19–20.)

Consider the implications of the publication date. As with primary sources, it is very important to understand the political, social, and cultural context in which a secondary source was produced. The original date of publication can provide clues about the historical questions and problems that interested historians writing in a particular time and place. If you are writing a historiographic essay (see 3d-2), reading secondary sources published in several different decades might offer a historical perspective on how interpretations of an issue or event have changed over time. Conversely, for some papers it may be important that you know the most recent theories about a historical subject. For example, a 2017 article reviewing theories about the construction of Native American burial mounds may contain more recent ideas than would a 1964 review. Do not assume, however, that newer interpretations are always better; some older works have contributed significantly to the field and may offer interpretations that are still influential. (As you become more experienced in historical research, you will be able to determine which older sources are still useful.)

Evaluate the logic of the author's argument. Any book or article makes an argument in support of a thesis. (For detailed information on what a thesis is, see 4c; for a discussion of how the thesis relates to the argument of a paper, see 4d.) Once you have identified the author's thesis, you should evaluate the evidence he or she uses to support it. You may not be in a position to judge the accuracy of the evidence, although you will build expertise as you continue to read about the subject. Nonetheless, you can evaluate the way in which the author uses the evidence he or she presents. You might ask yourself whether the evidence logically supports the author's point. For example, Margaret Sanger, who founded the American Birth Control League in 1921, was also involved in the U.S. eugenics movement, which advocated, among other things, for the sterilization of individuals deemed "mentally incompetent." This fact, however, does not justify the conclusion that *all* early-twentieth-century birth control advocates favored eugenics. Such an assertion would be a logical fallacy known as a *hasty generalization*.

You should also ask whether the same facts could be interpreted in another way to support a different thesis. For example, G. Stanley Hall, an early-twentieth-century

American psychologist, amassed evidence that demonstrated a correlation between a woman's educational level and the number of children she had: women who attended colleges and universities had fewer children than their less educated sisters. From this fact, he concluded that higher education caused sterility in women. A modern historian looking at the same evidence might conclude that education allowed women to become economically independent, freed them from the necessity of forming early marriages, and allowed them to pursue careers other than raising children.

Another consideration is whether the cause-and-effect relationships described in a source are legitimate. It may be true that event A happened before event B, but that does not necessarily mean that A caused B. For example, on July 20, 1969, Neil Armstrong became the first person to walk on the moon. The following winter was particularly harsh in the United States. We should not conclude, however, that the lunar landing caused a change in weather patterns. This would be a *post hoc* fallacy, from the Latin *post hoc, ergo propter hoc* ("after this, therefore because of this").

Finally, consider how the author deals with any counterevidence. (See 4d-2 for a discussion of counterevidence.)

Distinguish between popular and scholarly sources.   If you consult secondary sources for a history paper, it is important that you use scholarly, rather than popular, sources. Scholarly sources are written by experts in the field and are usually peer-reviewed—evaluated by other scholars— before being published. To determine whether a secondary source is scholarly or popular, consider the following questions.

- Does the author have academic credentials?
- Does the book or article have notes, a bibliography, and other academic apparatus?
- Is the source published by an academic press?
- Does the book or article analyze and interpret primary sources or the work of other scholars?

If you are still not sure whether a book or an article you want to use is an appropriate secondary source, consult your professor or a reference librarian.

Note: Although popular magazines are not appropriate *secondary* sources, they can be excellent *primary* sources for certain research topics. For example, you might consult back issues of *Time* magazine in order to explore how the news media covered the collapse of the Soviet Union, or you might examine the advertisements in *Good House-keeping* for a paper on women's economic importance in the period between the two world wars.

2b-3 Evaluating online sources

As noted above, the internet provides ready access to both primary and secondary sources. Editions of a wide variety of written primary sources (such as letters, treatises, and government publications) are available on the internet. Project Gutenberg (www.gutenberg.org), for example, is an extremely useful source for free e-books of interest to historians. You can also find a wide variety of visual sources — such as cartoons, photographs, images of antique maps, and other nonwritten primary sources — on the internet. YouTube (www.youtube .com), for example, is more than just a site for viewing music videos and Superbowl commercials; the site also offers radio and television addresses, newscasts, interviews, films, and other historically significant video materials.

If you are looking for secondary sources, historians may publish their research online in electronic journals like the *E-Journal of Portuguese History* (www.brown.edu /Departments/Portuguese_Brazilian_Studies/ejph); increasingly, some scholarly journals are published simultaneously in print and electronic formats. In addition, digitized versions of countless scholarly articles are available in electronic databases such as *JSTOR: The Scholarly Journal Archive* (www.jstor.org), which scans and archives a wide variety of scholarly print journals.

Websites maintained by universities, museums, government agencies, and other institutions can be a gold mine for students whose access to large research libraries is limited. Making effective use of the internet as a research tool, however, requires you to anticipate and avoid the special problems that it presents.

The most significant difficulty you may encounter when trying to evaluate a source accessed online is determining its credibility. When working with such a source, first determine if it has a print or real-life equivalent. Is it an article from a journal that is published in print? Is it an artifact that resides in a museum? If the source actually exists in physical form, you can refer to the Tips for

Writers boxes in 2b-1 and 2b-2 to help you study and evaluate it. If, however, the source exists only online, you must use extra caution in evaluating it. This is because, while articles in scholarly journals and books from academic presses are carefully reviewed by other scholars in the field, anyone with Internet access can create a website or a blog. You should also be aware that many popular online resources are not appropriate sources for scholarly research. For example, *Wikipedia*, the widely used online encyclopedia, is composed of entries written largely by anonymous authors. The entries are not peer-reviewed; moreover, anyone can modify a *Wikipedia* entry (although some pages attempt to prevent vandalism by allowing only registered users to make changes). It is worth noting, however, that *Wikipedia* entries often contain useful references and links to helpful online resources.

The questions in the Tips for Writers box on the next page will help you determine whether a website is reliable. In general, the most worthwhile sites with the most accurate sources will probably have a scholarly affiliation. You can find reputable sites by consulting your professor or a reference librarian.

Once you have determined that a website is credible, you *still* need to evaluate the material it contains. If you are using a primary source found on the website, analyze it using the criteria in the Tips for Writers box on page 13. If you are accessing an article or other secondary source, evaluate its usefulness and reliability by using the guidelines in the Tips for Writers box on page 18.

2b-4 Identifying fake news

Increasingly, people are turning to online sources, including social media, as their primary source for news and information about a wide range of topics. Unfortunately, this trend has been accompanied by an increase in fake news stories and websites. Trustworthy media outlets, whether print, broadcast, or online, adhere to a code of standards and ethics whose principles include accuracy, truthfulness, objectivity, and impartiality. When the editors of legitimate new sources wish to express their *opinions* about important issues, they do so on a clearly labeled editorial page. Most legitimate news sources also provide a variety of opinion pieces representing diverse points of view.

Tips for Writers
Questions for Evaluating Websites

- Is the author's identity clear? If so, what are his or her academic credentials? Does the author list an academic degree? Is he or she affiliated with a college or university? Do other web sites provide additional information about the author?

- Does the author provide evidence for his or her assertions, such as citations and bibliographies? Are the sources up-to-date? Does the author include the sources for statistics?

- Is the site affiliated with an academic institution, press, or journal? The web address—or URL—can provide some clues to such affiliations. If *.edu* or *.gov* appears in the address, the site is published by an educational or governmental institution, which should give you a greater degree of confidence in the material it contains.

- Is the site sponsored by a particular organization? (Look for *.org* in the URL.) Do you know anything about the interests and concerns of the person or group that publishes the site? (Check the home page or click on "About" to find a mission statement.) Does the organization seem biased?

- Does the site allow users to add or change content? If so, you cannot rely on the site to provide accurate information, even if it includes notes, references to academic sources, or useful links. (This is the case, for example, with *Wikipedia* articles, which often include scholarly apparatus but can typically be altered by any user.)

- What is the purpose of the site? Is it designed to inform? Persuade? Sell a product? Does the site contain advertising, and if so, does it affect the way the content is presented?

- Does the information on the site coincide with what you have learned about the subject from other sources?

- Has the site been updated recently?

- Does the site contain useful links to other sites? Are the linked sites affiliated with reputable institutions or persons?

If you are still unsure whether an online source is reliable, it is best to consult your professor or a reference librarian.

Despite these standards of journalistic integrity, legitimate news sources are not infallible; for example, the headline of the first edition of the *Chicago Daily Tribune* for November 3, 1948, boldly proclaimed "Dewey defeats Truman." Truman had, in fact, won handily. However, this famous mistake was not a deliberate attempt to deceive the public but, rather, reflected the near unanimous consensus of political analysts and polls at the time the first edition of the paper went to press—before all the results were in. The *Tribune* corrected the mistake in the next edition. Mistakes made by legitimate news sources should not be confused with "fake news." Fake news sources, unlike legitimate sources, deliberately try to mislead their readers and further a particular agenda by ignoring factual evidence, distorting the context of words or events, or simply making things up. The ability to determine whether a news source is reliable is thus an essential skill.

Ask the right questions.   Many of the same critical thinking questions that you would ask in evaluating primary, secondary, and other online sources can also help you determine whether a news story or source is reliable.

- Is the author of the article named? If so, what are his/her credentials? Can you verify the author's credentials through an independent search?
- Does the author provide evidence for the claims he/she makes by naming sources and providing links to source material that can be checked?
- Can the claims in the article be verified by an independent source or, better yet, by multiple independent sources?
- Does the article appear on a site or blog sponsored by a particular person, group, or organization? If so, does that person, group, or organization advocate for a particular political or social agenda or viewpoint? (Hint: You can often find this information on the "about" page.)
- Is there a date on the article and, if so, is it current?

Do some research.   Legitimate news sources have policies and practices in place that help to ensure that their reporting meets the standards established for journalistic integrity. Many news organizations publish these standards online; for example, you can find National Public Radio's code of standards—the *NPR Ethics Handbook*—at ethics.npr.org. Check to see if the news source in which you are interested has a published statement of journalistic standards by searching under "[name of organization] code of standards and ethics."

Use Fact-Checkers. There are several reliable online fact-checking sites that can help you to determine if a claim is legitimate or not. Some useful sites include:

- FactCheck.org. This is a nonpartisan, nonprofit project of the Annenberg Public Policy Center of the University of Pennsylvania, dedicated to determining the accuracy of statements made by politicians and other "political players." One section of this site, SciCheck, is devoted to checking the factual accuracy of scientific claims that might affect public policy decisions.
- Politifact.com. This is a Pulitzer Prize-winning site devoted to researching claims made by political figures.
- Snopes.com, established in 1995, is dedicated to verifying or debunking internet rumors, urban legends, and "news" stories of questionable origin.
- TinEye.com lets you do a reverse-image search to see if an image has appeared elsewhere. Using this tool will help you determine if a picture has been altered, taken out of context, or actually records a completely different event than that claimed by the site.

3

Approaching Typical Assignments in History

When students imagine the assignments they might receive in a history class, they often think about research papers, which will be discussed in detail in Chapter 5. However, history students are frequently given shorter writing assignments with which they may be less familiar: summaries and annotated bibliographies; short papers in which they analyze or compare primary sources; critiques of books or journal articles; historiographic essays; and film reviews. Each of these assignments is based on close, careful reading of one or more texts, and reading accurately, critically, and analytically is in itself a typical assignment in a history class. This chapter introduces you to the process of reading actively and discusses some typical writing assignments.

Note: Since the specifics of your assignment may vary from the examples in this chapter, you should always read your assignment carefully and consult your professor if you have questions.

3a Reading actively in history

Most scholars would agree that reading and writing are interrelated processes. As you read, you begin to see new connections among the ideas, people, and events you are studying. Then, as you start to write, new questions arise, prompting you to look at the texts you have already read in new ways and to find new materials that might help you answer your questions. History courses typically require a great deal of reading from a wide variety of sources; even nonwritten sources need to be critically analyzed or "read." Consequently, reading is the assignment you will encounter most frequently. If your professor has assigned a textbook, you will probably be expected to read a chapter or two each week. In addition, you may be asked to read a variety of secondary sources, including articles from scholarly journals or books about a particular aspect of your subject. Many professors also assign primary sources, documents ranging from medieval chronicles to legal documents to newspaper accounts. (For a fuller discussion of primary and secondary sources, including advice for evaluating nonwritten sources, see Chapter 2.) If you are writing a research paper, you will need to find, read, and analyze a variety of sources pertaining to your topic that are not part of the reading assigned to the whole class. Since reading is such an important assignment, it is essential to give serious consideration to how you read.

Reading for a history course is not like reading a best-selling novel for personal enjoyment; it is not enough to skim each page once and get the gist of the story. Similarly, you should avoid the common, but not very useful, habit of reading passively, plodding through a text line by line in hopes of absorbing some of the material it contains. To do your best work in history, you need to become an active reader. In contrast to passive readers, active readers are engaged in a dialogue with the text. They ask questions, make comments, and connect what they are reading to information they already know and texts they have already read. This kind of careful and critical reading is crucial both for active and intelligent participation in class discussion and for writing effective papers.

As you read in history, you must accomplish several tasks. Obviously, you need to understand the content, but you must also *evaluate* its usefulness, *analyze* its significance, and *synthesize* all of your reading into one coherent picture of the topic you are studying. The reading strategies described below will help you think critically about and analyze sources.

Pre-read the text.   Before you even begin to read, you should try to get a sense of the scope of the book or article and what it might tell you. If you are reading a book, note its subtitle, if any; examine the table of contents; check for appendices and lists of maps and/or illustrations.

If you are reading an article, look for an abstract at the beginning of the text and check for section headings. If you are examining a primary source, read the introduction to the text or the headnote to the document. For both books and articles, look at the bibliography and determine how extensive any footnotes or endnotes are. Spending a few minutes on such pre-reading tasks will help you determine how to approach your reading and consequently will make it more productive.

Determine the author's thesis.   Passive readers read as if everything a book or an article contains is equally important; following the advice of the King of Hearts in *Alice in Wonderland*, they "begin at the beginning, go on . . . to the end, then stop," picking up bits of information somewhat haphazardly as they go. Active readers begin by identifying the author's thesis—the conclusion that the author has reached as a result of his or her research and analysis. Since the argument of a book or an article is designed to demonstrate the thesis, understanding a source's main idea enables readers to absorb the text more effectively. (For additional information, see 4c.) The quickest way to identify an author's thesis is to read the preface, introduction, and conclusion of a book, or the first few paragraphs of an article. It is usually in these sections that an author states his or her main points. (Looking at the last chapter of a history book is not cheating, nor will it spoil the ending, unless you have been assigned a historical mystery, like Josephine Tey's novel *The Daughter of Time*.)

Read with the author's thesis in mind.   If you are reading a book or an article about a subject that is new to you, it is tempting to get caught up in the details and try to remember all of the facts. However, because the historian's goal is not simply to *collect* facts but to *organize* and *interpret* them in a way that allows us to better understand the people and societies of the past, it is much more useful to read a book or an article with an eye to understanding how an author builds an argument in support of his or her interpretation, or thesis. To do this, you should identify the main pieces of evidence the author cites in support of his or her conclusions. Often, the first sentence (or topic sentence) of the body paragraphs in an article or the introductory paragraphs of each chapter of a book will indicate the most important elements of an author's argument. (For more information, see 4d and 4e.)

Ask questions of the text.   As you read with the author's thesis in mind, you should constantly interrogate the text: What is the author's point here? Why has he or she chosen this example? Do you disagree with any points the author makes, and if so, why? As you try to answer these rather broad and general questions, new, more tightly focused and nuanced questions will arise, taking you deeper into the text. In this way, asking questions of the text helps you read with increasing sophistication and insight.

Write as you read.   Active readers are *physically* active, writing as they read. Writing while reading serves several functions. Writing directly in the margins of the text (provided, of course, that the text belongs to you) or highlighting pages in an e-book can help you locate important or confusing passages that you want to return to later. In addition, taking notes in your own words can help you remember what you have read and help you solidify your understanding of the text. Finally, writing as you read will help you clarify your thoughts about what you are reading and provide direction for further reading and research.

The writing you do while reading can take many different forms; some useful suggestions appear in the Tips for Writers box on page 30.

Review what you have written.   While writing itself helps many people remember what they have read, it is particularly useful to review your notes periodically. Make sure you have answered the questions that the reading raised for you and have compared the arguments of each text you are reading with the other readings for the class.

Read actively to prepare for class discussions.   Many history courses include participation as a component of the final grade. The suggestions for active reading in this chapter not only will allow you to get the most out of your reading but also will help you become an effective participant in class. Here are some specific suggestions for preparing for class discussions based on reading assignments.

- If your professor provides discussion questions, read through them first in order to get some idea of how to direct your reading.
- If possible, read the assigned text twice—once to get a general idea of the content and again to look

Tips for Writers
Writing as You Read

- Underline or highlight important points, including the thesis and topic sentences.

- Look up unfamiliar words in a dictionary, and write their definitions in the margins of the text, if it belongs to you, or create a working vocabulary list in a notebook or computer file.

- Talk back to the text by writing notations in the margins or in a separate document. Include questions you want to answer, disagreements you have with the author's argument, and cross-references to other materials you have read on the subject.

- Write summaries of your reading to ensure that you have understood the material. (See 3b-1 for advice on summaries.)

- Copy out, in quotation marks, any particularly striking phrases or statements that you might want to quote directly in your work, and note complete bibliographic information. (See 5d for further advice on effective note taking.) If you are "cutting and pasting" quotations from online sources, make sure you put quotation marks around any text you have copied and note the URL; that way, you will be able to distinguish your own notes from the text you are reading and avoid unintentional plagiarism.

- Always keep a record of the complete bibliographical information for *any* source you consult. If you are taking notes from online sources, make sure to record the URL *as you consult the source*, since websites can sometimes disappear.

- Keep a journal—in a notebook or on your computer—in which you can record any ideas, insights, or questions that occur to you as you read.

specifically for issues raised in previous classes or discussion questions.

- Write down page references for ideas or issues you want to discuss, quotations you would like to draw to the class's attention, or passages you found confusing or interesting. Class discussion is much richer if you can refer to specific places in the text as evidence for your assertions.

- Write down any questions you have while reading, and note any connections with other texts, images, and films that you have studied during the semester.

3b Writing about reading

As noted previously, writing summaries and recording complete bibliographical information for the sources you consult are useful techniques for reading in history. Some professors may even make these practices into formal assignments by requiring students to write a summary or compile an annotated bibliography.

3b-1 Summaries

History students are often required to read complex and difficult texts. As a result, many professors find it useful to have students write a summary, or *précis*, of a particularly challenging or complicated document, article, or section of a book.

Writing a summary requires you to condense what you have read and describe the author's central ideas in your own words; it helps ensure that you have understood and digested the material. A summary should not include your reaction to or critical analysis of the text. Rather, a summary should recount the author's main point, or thesis, and the key evidence (examples, illustrations, statistics, and so on) used to support it. You should not include *all* of the author's evidence; identifying the *most important* evidence is part of the challenge of writing a summary.

In writing your summary, it is essential that the wording and turns of phrase be entirely your own and not those of the text you are summarizing. To do otherwise is plagiarism, which is no more acceptable in a summary than in any other kind of writing. (For a detailed discussion of plagiarism and how to avoid it, see Chapter 6.)

3b-2 Annotated bibliographies

When you start to study an unfamiliar topic or begin to work on a research paper, you will need to identify and evaluate the materials that will enable you to develop an understanding of the general topic and what other scholars have said about it, and form your own interpretations of the sources. In other words, you will need to generate a bibliography.

A *bibliography* is a list of books and articles on a specific topic; it may include both primary and secondary sources. An *annotated bibliography* begins with the information included in a bibliography and then expands on it by including a brief summary of each book or article and assessing its value for the topic under discussion. An annotated bibliography, then, demonstrates your ability to gather, examine, and evaluate materials pertaining to a particular subject.

An annotated bibliography is an especially versatile and flexible assignment, so you should pay careful attention to the instructions provided by your professor. Regardless of the length or scope of the assignment, however, entries in an annotated bibliography generally follow a similar format. The entries should be arranged alphabetically by authors' last names. (See 7c-2 and 7c-3 for complete information about how to write bibliographic entries for a variety of sources.) Following the bibliographic information, you should include an *annotation*—a short paragraph in which you describe the content of the source and its usefulness for your topic. The following are some elements you might include in an annotation.

- A one-sentence description of what the book or article is about, including the author's thesis.
- A brief description of who the author is and what his or her credentials are.
- A brief description of the evidence the author uses to support his or her thesis.
- A concise evaluation of the author's use of sources and the validity of his or her argument.
- A brief description of the value of the book or article for your project.

Remember that entries in an annotated bibliography should be relatively short; you will not be able to write a full analysis of the book or article, as you would in a book review or critique (see 3d-1). Nevertheless, you should indicate the overall content of the source and its value for your project.

As noted above, each professor will have specific requirements for an annotated bibliography; the number of items, as well as the length of each entry, might vary dramatically from one instructor to the next, so it is important to follow your professor's instructions carefully. The following is one example of an annotated bibliography entry.

Fletcher, Richard. *The Cross and the Crescent: Christianity and Islam from Muhammad to the Reformation*. New York: Penguin/Viking, 2004.

This book examines the interactions, both positive and negative, between Christianity and Islam in the medieval and early modern periods. Fletcher, formerly a professor of medieval history at the University of York, England, argues that despite some productive interactions in the areas of trade and intellectual life, Christians and Muslims did not achieve any real measure of mutual understanding in the period under discussion. Rather, relations between the two cultures were marked by fear and hostility on the Christian side, and disdain and aloofness on the part of Muslims. Fletcher cites numerous examples to demonstrate that even in the most multicultural parts of the medieval world (Spain, Sicily, the Latin crusader states), Christians and Muslims "lived side by side, but did not blend" (p. 116). Although Fletcher's book is brief (161 pages), it is both scholarly and eminently readable, even for a nonspecialist, and provides a clearly argued introduction to the subject that elucidates both Muslim and Christian viewpoints. Footnotes enable the student to pursue the sources the author used, and a narrative bibliography provides suggestions for further reading. The book also includes a useful chronology.

3c Using primary sources

As noted in Chapter 2, primary sources constitute the basic materials of historical research. Because examining and interpreting primary sources is so fundamental to the historian's craft, many professors ask their students to write an analysis of a single source or an essay comparing two or more primary sources.

3c-1 Single-source analysis

A single-source paper can take many forms. You may be asked to analyze a book-length text, a shorter document such as a letter, an artifact such as a tribal mask, or an image such as a photograph. You may be assigned a particular source to analyze, or you may be allowed to write about a source of your choosing. Whatever the specifics of your assignment, a single-source analysis asks you to examine a primary source in depth, often without reference to the work of other historians, in order to determine what it can tell you about the people and the period you are studying.

To write an effective primary source analysis, you first need to ask questions about the nature of the source itself: Who wrote this document or made this artifact? When was this source created, and why? The questions for evaluating primary sources listed in the Tips for Writers boxes in Chapter 2, pages 13 and 14–15, will help you begin to think about the fundamental aspects of your source.

Once you have answered the basic questions about your source, however, you must go beyond simple description and discuss the *significance* of the source: What can it tell us about the person who wrote or made it, or the time and place in which he or she lived? Can the source tell us anything about the structures and norms of the author's society? What a source can tell you depends on both the nature of the source itself and the questions you ask of it. Think of yourself as a detective interrogating a witness who is not very forthcoming. The source you are analyzing can tell you quite a bit about the period and people you are studying, but not all of that information is obvious at first glance, and the "witness" might not volunteer everything it knows until you ask the right questions. In general, the quality of your source analysis will depend on the quality of the questions you ask; take enough time to read the document or examine the artifact carefully and extract from it every bit of information you can.

Example 1: Analyzing a written text

In the summer of 1925, a high school teacher named John Thomas Scopes was arrested in Dayton, Tennessee, for violating the Butler Act, a state law prohibiting the teaching of Darwin's theory of evolution in public schools. At the time, the issue of Scopes's guilt or innocence quickly faded into the background. Instead, the public's deep fascination with the trial — which was quickly dubbed the "trial of the century" — was attributable to the larger-than-life personalities and reputations of the two lead attorneys: Clarence Darrow, the well-known champion of unpopular civil liberties causes, for the defense; and William Jennings Bryan, the fundamentalist "great commoner" and three-time Democratic presidential candidate, for the prosecution. On the seventh day of the trial, the defense, in an unexpected and unprecedented move, called Bryan to the stand as an "expert witness" on the Bible. Astonishingly, Bryan agreed to testify.

Imagine that you have been given the following assignment.

> The following is an excerpt from the transcript of the seventh day of the Scopes trial, during which Darrow questioned Bryan about the creation of the earth. Your assignment is to write a short (two-page) paper analyzing the interaction between Bryan and Darrow and evaluating the impact of their beliefs and personalities on the trial.
>
> *Darrow:* Do you think the earth was made in six days?
>
> *Bryan:* Not six days of twenty-four hours.
>
> *Darrow:* Doesn't it say so?
>
> *Bryan:* No, sir.
>
> *Prosecuting attorney A. Thomas Stewart:* I want to interpose another objection. What is the purpose of this examination?
>
> *Bryan:* The purpose is to cast ridicule on everybody who believes in the Bible, and I am perfectly willing that the world shall know that these gentlemen have no other purpose than ridiculing every Christian who believes in the Bible.
>
> *Darrow:* We have the purpose of preventing bigots and ignoramuses from controlling the education of the United States and you know it, and that is all. . . .
>
> *Bryan:* . . . I am simply trying to protect the word of God against the greatest atheist or agnostic in the United States! (Prolonged applause.) I want the papers to know I am not afraid to get on the stand in front of him and let him do his worst! I want the world to know! (Prolonged applause.)[1]

Although this document is relatively short, an effective analysis would include several steps.

Examine the nature of the source. In analyzing any document, you should begin by asking questions about the nature of the source.

- When was this source created, and why?
- What kinds of information can be found in a trial transcript?

1. Jeffrey P. Moran, *The Scopes Trial: A Brief History with Documents* (Boston: Bedford/St. Martin's, 2002), 156.

- Does the transcript record anything other than dialogue?

For other kinds of documents, you might ask questions about the author and his or her intended audience. (For advice on evaluating primary sources, see 2b-1 and the Tips for Writers box on p. 13.)

Focus your analysis on the assignment.   Since the assignment focuses on Darrow and Bryan, you then need to think about what the transcript can tell us about their personalities, their understanding of the meaning of the trial, and their relationship to each other.

The assignment first asks you to analyze the interaction between Bryan and Darrow.

- How does Darrow see Bryan? Is the tone of his questioning neutral? Respectful? Hostile? What adjectives does he use to characterize Bryan and his views?
- How does Bryan see Darrow? Is the tone of his responses neutral? Respectful? Hostile? What adjectives does he use to characterize Darrow and his views?

The assignment then asks you to evaluate the impact of their beliefs and personalities on the trial.

- What can we determine from the transcript about the demeanor and behavior of Bryan and Darrow?
- What does Darrow see as the central issue of the trial?
- What does Bryan see as the central issue?
- Whom does Bryan see as his audience? Is he speaking to the judge? To the audience in the courtroom? To a wider audience?
- To whom is Darrow speaking? Is he addressing his questions primarily to Bryan, or to a wider audience?

Consider what the document reveals about the wider historical context.   Although the interaction between Bryan and Darrow is the dominant aspect of this text, the document also provides some hints about what those who witnessed their confrontation thought about it, which could provide us with a view into the norms of society at the time.

- How does the audience in the courtroom react to Bryan's testimony? Do they support Bryan or Darrow?

- What does the audience's response suggest about the prevailing attitude toward evolution in Dayton at the time?
- Why does prosecuting attorney A. Thomas Stewart object to the line of questioning taken by Darrow? Why might he see this entire line of questioning as irrelevant?

Answering these questions will help you think about and analyze the source. Then you will need to organize your answers into an essay. Keep in mind that a source analysis is not a summary. Rather, a single-source analysis, like any other history paper, should focus on a thesis. The essay should include an introduction; several body paragraphs that present the evidence that supports your thesis; and a conclusion. (For detailed advice on how to write an effective history paper, see Chapter 4.)

Example 2: Analyzing a visual source

In August of 1588, King Philip II of Spain launched a fleet of one hundred and thirty ships — the Spanish Armada — against his mortal enemy, Queen Elizabeth I of England. The English fleet, while smaller, had faster and more maneuverable ships carrying more powerful guns. Ultimately, having incurred heavy damage, the defeated Spanish commanders made the fateful decision to sail up the English Channel into the North Atlantic, where a storm decimated what was left of the fleet; less than half of the armada managed to limp home.

Imagine that you have been given the following assignment.

> This is one of three versions of a portrait of Queen Elizabeth I celebrating the defeat of the Spanish Armada; the artist is unknown, but it is believed that this version was commissioned by Sir Francis Drake. It is usually described as an allegory; that is, it is not just a portrait, but, rather, contains symbols and images that convey a political and moral story. Your assignment is to write a short (two-page) paper analyzing what this portrait can tell us about how the English viewed the meaning and significance of the defeat of the Spanish Armada.

An effective analysis would include several elements.

Consider the nature of the source. While the artist is unknown, you can still ask questions about the circumstances of its creation.

English School/Getty Images

- Who was Sir Francis Drake?
- What was his relationship to Queen Elizabeth?
- What role did he play in the defeat of the Armada?
- Why might he have wanted a copy of this portrait?

Consider the painting in its historical context.   Although the painting is an allegory, it still reflects real historical events.

- Elizabeth sits in front of two depictions of the Spanish Armada. What story are these two images designed to tell? To what extent do these images reflect the historical reality of the event?
- England and Spain were rivals in the Atlantic world and the Americas. What does this portrait suggest about that rivalry? What does the painting imply about the relationship between the defeat of the Armada and England's empire in the Americas? What claim is being made here?

Consider the elements of the painting.   The assignment tells you that art historians consider this painting an allegory; you should therefore carefully analyze the content and composition of the painting.

- Elizabeth styled herself "the Virgin Queen." In this portrait, she is wearing many pearls, which were symbols of virginity. What does this portrayal of Elizabeth suggest about how she was viewed as a monarch? What might it suggest about her relationship to God? What might it suggest about her relationship to her people?

- A storm is raging in the painting above Elizabeth's left shoulder. What is the significance of the fact that she is facing away from the storm?
- Elizabeth's hand is placed on a globe; specifically, she is touching the Americas. What is the significance of this detail?
- Above the globe is England's imperial crown. What does this image suggest about the relationship between England and Spain?
- Considering these symbols as a group, what is the political or moral point behind this allegory?

Your answers to these questions will form the basis for your essay. As with an analysis of a written source, your final paper should be focused on a thesis and supported by evidence from the source. (See Chapter 4 for detailed advice on how to organize and write a history paper.)

3c-2 Comparative papers

A second kind of primary-source paper that you might be asked to write in a history course is one in which you compare two or more sources. In a comparative paper, you start by evaluating and analyzing each source individually, as for a single-source analysis. Keep in mind, however, that a successful comparative paper is not a series of mini-essays on each source glued together. Instead, you need to consider how the sources relate to one another: How are they similar? How are they different? You also need to consider the *significance* of those similarities and differences, by far the most important element in a comparative paper. The danger of compare/contrast essays is the tendency to compile "laundry lists" of similarities and differences without a central point or argument. To avoid this problem, focus your paper on a thesis statement that reflects your conclusion about what the similarities and differences in the sources can tell us.

An example

The Scopes trial received daily coverage by the media in cities throughout the United States and was the first trial to be nationally broadcast live on radio. Hundreds of reporters descended on the quiet southern town of Dayton. Imagine that you have been given the following assignment.

> The following document is an excerpt from the *New York Times*'s coverage of the seventh day of the trial, as it appeared in the paper on July 21, 1925. Compare this article with the actual trial transcript (see p. 35) and write a short (two- to three-page) paper evaluating the *Times*'s coverage of the dramatic events of day seven.

> So-called Fundamentalists of Tennessee sat under the trees of the Rhea County Court House lawn today listening to William J. Bryan defend his faith in the "literal inerrancy" of the Bible, and laughed. . . . The greatest crowd of the trial had come in anticipation of hearing Messrs. Bryan and Darrow speak, and it got more than it expected. It saw Darrow and Bryan in actual conflict—Mr. Darrow's rationalism in combat with Mr. Bryan's faith—and forgot for the moment that Bryan's faith was its own. . . . There was no pity for the helplessness of the believer come so suddenly and unexpectedly upon a moment when he could not reconcile statements of the Bible with generally accepted facts. There was no pity for his admissions of ignorance of things boys and girls learn in high school. . . . These Tennesseans were enjoying a fight. That an ideal of a great man, a biblical scholar, an authority on religion, was being dispelled seemed to make no difference. They grinned with amusement and expectation. . . . And finally, when Mr. Bryan, pressed harder and harder by Mr. Darrow, confessed he did not believe everything in the Bible should be taken literally, the crowd howled.[2]

As with a single-source analysis, an effective comparative essay will require several steps.

Examine the nature of the sources. In order to compare the two documents, begin by evaluating each source individually. Questions analyzing the trial transcript can be found on pages 35–36. For the newspaper source, consider the following questions.

- When was the source written, and why?
- What do we know about the political leanings of the *New York Times* in 1925? Was it conservative? Liberal? Neutral?

2. *New York Times*, July 21, 1925, in Jeffrey P. Moran, *The Scopes Trial: A Brief History with Documents* (Boston: Bedford/St. Martin's, 2002), 161.

- Who read the *Times*, and what political, social, or economic groups did these readers represent?

Focus your analysis on the assignment. Since the assignment asks you to compare the two sources, you should consider both the similarities and the differences in the sources and how the sources relate to each other.

First, the assignment asks you to compare this article with the actual trial transcript.

- Do the sources agree on any details that would enable us to determine what happened?
- How does the *Times* describe Darrow's demeanor and characterize his views? Is this depiction consistent with the evidence of the trial transcript? Where do the sources differ, and what is the significance of these differences?
- How does the *Times* describe Bryan's demeanor and characterize his views? Is this depiction consistent with the evidence of the trial transcript? Where do the sources differ, and what is the significance of these differences?

The assignment also asks you to evaluate the *Times*'s coverage of the dramatic events of day seven.

- Does the newspaper article accurately reflect the confrontation of Darrow and Bryan as depicted in the trial transcript? Where do the accounts differ?
- Is the author of the *Times* article objective, or does he have a detectable bias? What aspects of his reporting indicate what his bias might be?
- How are the spectators described in the sources? Do they support Bryan or Darrow? How can we account for the difference in the way they are depicted in the two documents?

As with a single-source analysis, your answers to these questions will form the building blocks of your comparative essay. As with any other history paper, you will need to advance a thesis in your introduction, support the thesis in the body of your paper with evidence from the texts, and end with a conclusion that ties everything together. (For more on writing an effective history paper, see Chapter 4.)

Tips for Writers
Writing a Comparative Essay

- Give approximately equal weight to each source.
- Consider both similarities and differences.
- Focus your essay on a thesis that addresses the significance of the similarities and differences you have noted; avoid compiling a "laundry list."
- Support your thesis by citing specific evidence from the text, using quotations where appropriate.

3d Using secondary sources

While primary sources are the basic materials with which historians work, secondary sources—books and articles in which historians analyze and interpret primary sources in order to reconstruct some aspect of the past—are also extremely valuable for studying history. Professors sometimes ask their students to read, evaluate, and write about the work of professional historians. Two typical assignments that ask you to write about secondary sources are critiques or book reviews and historiographic essays.

3d-1 Critiques and book reviews

To demonstrate your ability to read a text critically and analytically, you may be asked to critique an article or review a book (a book review is simply a critique of a full-length book). You may feel unqualified to complete such an assignment; after all, the author of the text is a professional historian. However, even if you cannot write from the same level of experience and knowledge as the author, you can write an effective review if you understand what the assignment requires. Reviews and critiques of texts begin with careful, active, and critical reading. (See 3a for advice on reading critically.) Active reading requires you to keep the author's thesis in mind, note the evidence used to support that thesis, ask the critical questions for evaluating sources outlined in Chapter 2, and note your reactions and responses to the text as you go. Your review or critique then grows out of this active reading.

A review or critique is not the same thing as a book report, which simply summarizes the content of a book. Nor does a review or critique merely report your reaction (for example, "This book was boring" or "I liked this article"). Rather, when writing a review or critique, you not only report on the content of the text and your response to it but also assess its strengths and weaknesses. So, for example, it is not enough to say "This book is not very good"; you need to explain and/or justify your reaction through an analysis of the text. Did you find the book unconvincing because the author did not supply enough evidence to support his or her assertions? Is the logic faulty? Or did you disagree with the book's underlying assumptions? Finally, note that *critical* does not mean "negative." If a book is well written and presents an original thesis supported by convincing evidence, say so. A good book review does not have to be negative; it does have to be fair and analytical. (Incidentally, when you are writing your critique or review, it is unnecessary to preface statements with *I think* or *in my opinion* since readers assume that as a reviewer you are expressing your own opinions.)

Though there is no one correct way to structure a critique or review, the following is a possible approach.

- Summarize the book or article, and relate the author's main point, or thesis. Make sure you briefly identify the author and note his or her credentials.

- Describe the author's viewpoint and purpose for writing; note any aspects of the author's background that are important for understanding the text.

- Note the most important evidence the author presents to support his or her thesis.

- Evaluate the author's use of evidence and describe how he or she deals with counterevidence. (See 4d-2 for a discussion of counterevidence.) Is the argument convincing?

- Compare this text with other books or articles you have read on the same subject.

- Conclude with a final evaluation of the book or article. You might discuss who would find it useful and why.

Note: While many of the elements of a review or critique are the same as those found in an annotated bibliography entry, full-length book reviews and article critiques should be much longer and more detailed than brief bibliography entries.

3d-2 Historiographic essays

As noted in Chapter 1, historians frequently disagree about how to interpret the events they study. For example, some historians have interpreted the Magna Carta, a charter signed by King John of England in 1215, as a revolutionary declaration of fundamental individual freedoms; others have seen it as a conservative restatement of feudal privilege. These differences in interpretation reflect the varying approaches that historians take to their subject. For example, individual historians might be interested primarily in social, cultural, political, economic, legal, or intellectual history. They might approach their work from a Marxist, Freudian, feminist, or postmodernist point of view. Such orientations and affiliations affect the ways in which historians explore and interpret the past; thus, historians interested in the same historical event might examine different sets of sources to answer the same question. For example, in studying the causes of the French Revolution, Marxist historians might focus on economic and class issues, while intellectual historians might concentrate on how the writings of the *philosophes* (a group of French Enlightenment writers) affected political thought and practice. Moreover, since the historian's work is embedded in a particular social and cultural context, historical interpretations and methodologies change over time. For example, the growth of the civil rights and feminist movements in the 1960s led to a greater interest in African American and women's history. To make students aware of a variety of interpretations and allow them to enter the exciting world of historical discussion and debate, some instructors ask their students to write historiographic essays.

A historiographic essay is one in which the writer, acting as a historian, studies the approaches to a topic that other historians have taken. When you write a historiographic essay, you identify, compare, and evaluate the viewpoints of two or more historians writing on the same subject. Such an essay can take several forms. You might be asked, for example, to study the work of historians who lived during or near the time in which a particular event happened—for example, to explore the ways in which contemporary Chinese historians wrote about the Boxer Rebellion. A different kind of historiographic essay might require that you look at the ways in which historians have treated the same topic over time.

For example, to examine how historians have treated Thomas Jefferson, you might begin with two pre–Civil War biographies—Matthew L. Davis's *Memoirs of Aaron Burr* (1836–37), which provides a scathing critique of Jefferson, and Henry S. Randall's contrastingly positive *Life of Jefferson* (1858)—and end with the most recent studies of Jefferson. Yet another such assignment might ask you to compare the views of historians from several historical schools on the same event. You might, for example, be asked to compare Whig and Progressive interpretations of the American Revolution or Marxist and feminist views of the French Revolution. Historiographic essays may be short or quite lengthy. In any case, a historiographic essay focuses attention not on a historical event itself but rather on how historians have interpreted that event.

A historiographic essay combines some of the features of a book review with those of a short essay or research paper. You should begin with a critical reading of the texts containing historians' interpretations, keeping in mind the questions you would need to answer if you were going to write book reviews about them (see 3d-1). You should not, however, treat the historiographic essay as two or three book reviews glued together. Rather, you should synthesize your material and construct an argument in support of a thesis. The following thesis is from a student's essay on historians' interpretations of the colonial period of African history.

> Historians have held dramatically different views about the importance of European colonial rule in Africa: Marxist historians, along with others who focus on economic issues, have tended to see the colonial period as an important turning point, while cultural historians have maintained that the impact of the West on the ancient cultural traditions of Africa was superficial.

In the rest of the paper, the student supports the thesis as he or she would do in any other history paper. (For a fuller discussion of formulating and supporting a thesis, see 4c and 4d.)

3e Writing about film

While historians rely primarily on written texts, film and other visual texts have become increasingly important historical sources. Watching a film, like reading a book, should not be a passive exercise. If you use a film as a historical source, you need to approach or "read" it with the same critical and analytical skills that you would apply to a written text. Just as there are different kinds of written texts, so too are there different kinds of films. The most common types of films historians use are documentaries and feature films. Identifying which type of film you are dealing with is the essential first step in writing a film review.

Documentaries

Documentaries are films that use primary sources (such as photographs, paintings, and documents) and commentaries on those sources by various authorities (such as historians, biographers, and eyewitnesses) to construct a narrative of a historical figure or event. For this reason, documentaries should be considered secondary sources. Ken Burns's series *The Civil War*, which uses primary sources such as documents and photographs as well as commentary from historians, is a good example of this type of film.

Documentaries about events of the twentieth and twenty-first centuries are able to make use of a unique primary source: *footage*. Footage is a direct film, videotape, or digital recording of an event. Footage can be produced by professionals, such as television news videographers, or by amateurs, like Abraham Zapruder's 8 mm film of the assassination of John F. Kennedy. Footage is a primary source since it records events as they happen.

A documentary filmmaker's use of primary sources such as footage must be viewed critically. Filmmakers, like writers, choose what to record, usually with a particular purpose, and sometimes with a particular audience, in mind. Moreover, footage that makes its way to a news broadcast has been cut and edited. In evaluating a documentary that uses footage, try to determine why and by whom the original footage was shot and whether and for what purposes it has been edited.

Feature films

Feature films are films designed primarily as entertainment. They sometimes feature famous actors and always aim at box-office success. Historical rigor is usually not their primary concern, so we should not be surprised to find that such films vary dramatically in the accuracy with which they depict the period, events, and historical figures they ostensibly portray. At one end of the spectrum are films like *The Return of Martin Guerre*, which is based on a true story about a peasant who abandoned his family and the impostor who successfully took his place. The director, Daniel Vigne, consulted historical documents, attempted to faithfully re-create the material culture of the period, and made extensive use of historian Natalie Zemon Davis as a consultant. Consequently, this film might be considered a secondary source for our understanding of French peasant life in seventeenth-century France. By contrast, in his 1916 film *Joan the Woman*, legendary director Cecil B. DeMille took serious liberties with the historical accounts of Joan of Arc, inventing a love interest for her and linking her story with the English efforts against the Germans in France during World War I. DeMille's film has virtually no value as a secondary source for the history of Joan of Arc, but it is a valuable primary source for understanding American attitudes toward the Great War and the role of filmmakers in encouraging the United States to join the conflict. This points to an important consideration: all feature films can be viewed as primary sources for the cultural and social history of the period in which they were made.

Because of the growing importance of film of all sorts, writing a film review is an increasingly common assignment. The suggestions provided in 3d-1 for writing a critique or book review also apply to a film review. In addition, you should do the following.

- Determine whether the film is a documentary or a feature film. Who is the intended audience, and for what reason was the film made?
- If the film is a documentary, note the academic credentials of the experts who provide the commentary. If it is a feature film, determine whether the filmmaker made use of professional historians as consultants.
- For documentaries and feature films, analyze the interests and concerns of the producer, director, and screenwriter. Note any other films they have produced, directed, or written that might help the viewer understand their interests and biases. In this context, it is useful to determine whether the people most responsible for the film have provided interviews or written commentary that might shed light on their work. DVDs sometimes include

features such as interviews with the film's writer or director, interviews with consultants, and other materials that might help you understand the filmmaker's intentions and practices.

- Examine how the images presented in the film enhance our understanding of the subject and the period. Do the costumes and sets accurately portray the historical reality of the period? Does the film help us understand the material culture of the period?

- Analyze the cinematic techniques used to convey the story. Is the film shot in black and white or in color? How does the filmmaker use lighting to convey a mood or to make a symbolic point? How is one set of images juxtaposed with another to create an impression? What kinds of camera angles are used, and why?

- Analyze how the filmmaker uses sound. What kind of music is used in the soundtrack? Was it composed specifically for the film, or are classical or popular pieces used?

- Discuss the ways in which the filmmaker shapes the narrative. From what point of view is the story told? Does the film employ flashbacks or narrative voice-overs?

- If the film is based on a play or a specific text, compare the film with the original source. Are any themes or concepts portrayed more effectively in the film than in the text? Conversely, are any elements of the source eliminated or distorted in the film?

- Compare the film with other films, books, and articles on the same subject.

3f   Taking history exams

History exams reflect your ability to synthesize the materials you have examined over the course of a semester into a coherent picture of the period you are studying. If you have been attending classes and reading actively and critically throughout the semester, the final exam should not be an occasion for panic but rather a chance to demonstrate your understanding of the people, events, and institutions you have been studying.

3f-1   Preparing for an exam

The best preparation for an exam does not begin the day, or even the week, before the exam but takes place throughout the semester. Careful reading of the texts and periodic review of your notes will ensure that you have a firm grasp of the material come exam time. Throughout the semester, you should practice the following strategies.

Attend class regularly and take good notes. When taking notes, listen for the main points and note the evidence given to support those points. (You will discover that your professor's lectures usually follow the same format as a good essay.) Follow the same suggestions for a discussion class; your classmates will often make important points about the material you are studying.

Review your notes regularly, preferably after each class. If you review your notes while the class is fresh in your mind, it will be easier for you to notice places where you have not fully understood the material. Clarify confusing points as soon as possible.

Keep a list of important ideas, people, and events. How do you know which items to include on this list? Some will be obvious; if you are taking a course called Twentieth-Century Dictators, you should be able to identify Hitler, Mussolini, and Stalin. In cases in which the importance of a person or an idea is not so obvious, look for other clues: words that are italicized in your texts; concepts that recur in several of your readings; and terms, events, or people that your professor has highlighted for you or written on the board.

Refer to your syllabus throughout the semester. Many instructors provide detailed syllabi that state the themes for each section of the course. Use the syllabus as a guide for your own studying and thinking about the course material.

Take careful notes on the readings. Read with a notebook or computer at hand, and take notes as you read where you have not fully understood the material. (See 3b-1 for a fuller discussion.) Make sure to include page references in your notes.

The week before the exam, you should do the following.

- Review your notes, syllabus, and texts. Identify the most important themes and issues of the course, and assemble the evidence that clarifies those themes.
- Anticipate questions; if you were the professor, what questions would you ask?

3f-2 Answering identification questions

Professors often use identification questions as a way of testing your basic understanding of the material covered in the course. You may be asked to identify people, places, or events, or to define important concepts. If you have kept a running list of significant individuals, events, and terms, you probably will not be surprised by any of the items in the identification section of your test.

Students tend to make one of two mistakes in answering identification questions. On the one hand, they may produce answers that are too detailed. The response to an identification question should not be a fully developed, multipage essay. Often, your professor will tell you how long your response should be; you might, for example, be asked to write one sentence or a three- or four-sentence paragraph.

On the other hand, take care not to write too little. Your answer should be detailed enough to identify the individual person, event, or concept. For example, identifying Anne Boleyn as an English queen is clearly not enough; dozens of people can be identified as English queens. A more successful response would identify Anne Boleyn as the English queen who was the second wife of King Henry VIII and the mother of Queen Elizabeth I.

3f-3 Taking an essay exam

The essays you write for an exam will necessarily be shorter than the papers you write for your course, but they should follow the same basic format. In other words, an exam essay should begin with a thesis stated clearly in the first paragraph, followed by several paragraphs in which you provide evidence supporting your thesis, and end with a conclusion. (For detailed advice on writing a history essay, see Chapter 4.) The difficulty, of course, is that you will be writing this essay under pressure, in a limited period of time, and without the opportunity to check the accuracy of your data. The following are some suggestions for writing a successful essay on a history exam.

Preparing to write. *Do not begin to write right away.* This is probably the biggest mistake that students make in essay exams. Before you write, do the following.

- Read the exam carefully. Make sure you understand what each question is really asking. You will not gain points by scribbling down everything you know about the development of Chinese politics from the tenth century through the fifteenth century when the question asks you to discuss the impact of the Mongol invasion in 1260.

- If you are offered a choice, make sure you answer the question you can answer best. This may not always be the one you are drawn to first. One great insight about the significance of the Treaty of Waitangi will not be enough to write a good essay about Maori-British relations in nineteenth-century New Zealand. Be sure that you can cite several pieces of evidence in support of your thesis.

- Take the time to organize your thoughts. Jot down a quick outline for your essay, stating the thesis and listing the evidence you will provide to support that thesis.

Writing the essay. Once you are ready to write, your essay should follow the same format as any other history essay.

- Begin by writing an introductory paragraph that includes your thesis. Do not waste time restating the question; your professor knows what he or she asked.

- Make sure each subsequent paragraph focuses on one central idea that supports your thesis, and state this idea in the first, or topic, sentence. Follow the topic sentence with supporting evidence.

- If you are aware of any counterevidence, make sure you discuss it. (See 4d-2 for a discussion of counterevidence and how to deal with it.)

- Be sure to stick to the point. Do not go off on interesting tangents that are irrelevant to the question. Referring frequently to your outline will help keep you on track.

- Tie your essay together by stating your conclusions.

4

Following Conventions of Writing in History

Each academic discipline has its own practices, or conventions, that people writing in the discipline follow when engaged in a scholarly dialogue. Following the conventions for writing in history will make it easier for you to participate in an academic conversation in your field. Moreover, many historians are excellent stylists. Your instructor will pay attention to your writing, so your attempts to learn and follow the conventions of the discipline will be noticed—and worth the effort.

History students are most often asked to write two types of papers: short essays and research papers. Unlike most of the assignments described in Chapter 3, such papers often require you to examine *multiple* sources. Writing a historical essay is a process of synthesis—pulling together different sources, thinking about their relationship, and drawing conclusions about what, taken together, they can tell you about your subject. This chapter provides advice on all aspects of writing short essays—relatively brief papers with limited sources and, frequently, an assigned topic. The techniques outlined here are also the fundamental skills you will need for writing a full-fledged research paper, which is described in more detail in Chapter 5.

4a Approaching a history assignment

When faced with the task of writing a short essay in history, you must first analyze the assignment carefully, making sure to identify and understand *all* of its parts so that you know exactly what you are being asked to do. Some assignments include very specific and detailed directions, but in many cases the instructor's expectations will be implied, not explicit. To ensure that you fully understand your assignment, you should always do the following.

Determine the key verb. Most assignments include a key verb that will let you know how your instructor expects you to approach the essay. The following example is from a course on the history of Christian-Muslim relations.

> Compare the ways in which Fulcher of Chartres (a medieval Christian historian) and Ibn al-Athir (a medieval Muslim historian) explain the Christian success at the siege of Antioch during the First Crusade.

The operative word in the assignment is *compare*. Other assignments may ask you to *trace* the causes or *assess* the importance of a historical event. The key verb tells you how to structure your essay. For instance, an assignment that requires you to *compare* two or more texts, like the example given above, implies that you should give approximately equal weight to each of the sources included in your assignment, consider not only similarities but also differences, and come to some conclusion about the *significance* of the similarities and differences you have identified.

Determine what sources you should or may use. Short-paper assignments usually include specific instructions about which sources you should consider and, sometimes, which ones you may not. You might, for example, be instructed to consider *only* a specific set of newspaper articles or to develop your own interpretation of an artifact without reference to additional secondary sources. Always make sure you understand and follow these instructions.

Analyze and synthesize your sources. When you write a paper, you must, of course, begin by evaluating and analyzing each source you are using, following the advice given in Chapters 2 and 3. For the assignment given above, for instance, you would need to understand what both Fulcher of Chartres *and* Ibn al-Athir thought about the siege of Antioch.

Analyzing each source, though, is not sufficient; you also need to synthesize the information in your sources. When you use several sources as a means for interpreting a historical event, you should take care to integrate evidence from each source throughout your paper. An essay for the above assignment, for example, should *not* take the form of two mini-papers—one on Fulcher and one on Ibn al-Athir—glued together. Rather, it should examine the two sources *as they relate to each other*. You might discover, for example, that Fulcher and Ibn al-Athir agree that the gates to the city were opened for the Christian army by a Muslim cuirass-maker but that they differ in their interpretation of this event: Ibn al-Athir reports that the traitor succumbed to bribery, while Fulcher maintains that his actions were the result of three divine visions.

Finally, keep in mind that underlying every essay assignment in history is the question "Why is this important?" In the sample assignment, the instructor's expectation is that the student will not only analyze both sources and identify their similarities and differences but also draw conclusions about the *meaning* of those similarities and differences and explain why they are *significant*. You might note, for example, that the two texts provide very different perspectives on causation in history: the Christian historian ascribes almost everything that happened during the siege to the direct action of God, whereas the Muslim historian explains the same events without reference to divine intervention. One approach to writing this essay, then, might be to consider the degree to which medieval authors from different religious cultures shared a common set of beliefs about the world: What ideas do they share, and how and why do their worldviews differ? (For more information on writing a comparative essay, see 3c-2.)

Stay on topic.   Be careful to write about the topic that has actually been assigned. In reading Fulcher and Ibn al-Athir, for example, you may discover that both authors discuss the importance of Jerusalem in their respective religions. Although this is an interesting and important topic, it is not the subject of the assignment.

4b   Thinking like a historian

Before you begin to write your essay, you need to become familiar with a number of conventions that historians have established to govern their relationship with their subject; in other words, you need to learn how to think like a historian. Learning these conventions will enable you to be an active participant in historical conversations.

Respect your subject. When you write a history paper, you are forming a relationship of sorts with real people and events whose integrity must be respected. The people who lived in the past were not necessarily more ignorant or cruel (or, conversely, more innocent or moral) than we are. It is condescending, for example, to suggest that intelligent or insightful individuals, such as Galileo or Marie Curie, were "ahead of their time" (suggesting, of course, that they thought the same way we do and that their contemporaries were unintelligent). Similarly, it violates the conventions of historical thinking to dismiss individuals such as Renaissance astrologers or the author of the *Malleus Maleficarum*, a famous witch-hunting manual, as "backward" or "unenlightened" because their ideas or behaviors do not conform to our own standards or beliefs.

Do not generalize. Remember that groups are formed of individuals. Do not assume that everyone who lived in the past believed the same things or behaved the same way. Avoid broad generalizations such as "the medieval period was an age of faith" or "pre-modern people were not emotionally attached to their children." At best, such statements are clichés. More often than not, they are also wrong. (For more on the issue of appropriate language, see 4g-1.)

Avoid anachronism. An anachronistic statement is one in which an idea, event, person, or thing is represented in a way that is not consistent with its proper historical time or context. For example, the statement "Despite the fact that bubonic plague can be controlled with antibiotics, medieval physicians treated their patients with ineffective folk remedies," includes two anachronisms. First, although antibiotics are effective against bubonic plague, they had not yet been discovered in the fourteenth century; it is anachronistic to mention them in a discussion of the Middle Ages. Second, it is anachronistic to judge medieval medicine by modern standards. A more effective discussion of the medieval response to the bubonic plague would focus on fourteenth-century knowledge about health and disease, theories of contagion, and sanitation practices. In short, you should not import the values, beliefs, and practices of the present into the past. Try to understand the people and events of the past in their own contexts.

Be aware of your own biases.   We naturally choose to write about subjects that interest us. Historians should not, however, let their own concerns and biases direct the way they interpret the past. A student of early modern Europe, for example, might be dismayed by the legal, social, and economic limitations placed on women in that period. Reproaching sixteenth-century men for being "selfish and chauvinistic" might forcefully express such a student's sense of indignation about what appears to modern eyes as unjust, but it is not a useful approach for the historian, who tries to understand the viewpoints of people in the past in the social context of the period under study.

4c   Developing a thesis

Your *topic* is the subject you have been assigned to write about (for example, the Salem witchcraft trials, the Lewis and Clark expedition, the rise of the Nazi Party). If you merely collect bits of information about your topic, however, you will not have written an effective history paper. A history paper, like many other kinds of academic writing, usually takes the form of an argument in support of a *thesis*—a statement that reflects the *conclusion* you have reached about your topic after a careful analysis of the sources.

Since the thesis is the central idea that drives a history essay, it is important that you understand exactly what a thesis is. Imagine that you have been given the following essay assignment.

> Discuss the role of nonviolent resistance in the Indian independence movement.

As you develop your thesis statement, keep the following in mind.

- **A thesis is *not* a description of your paper topic.** Although your reader should not have to guess what your paper is about, the thesis must do more than announce your subject or the purpose for which you are writing. "This paper is about the role of nonviolent resistance in the Indian independence movement" is *not* a thesis statement; nor is "The purpose of this paper is to describe the methods Mohandas Gandhi used to gain India's independence from Great Britain." These sentences merely restate the assigned topic.

- **A thesis is *not* a question.** Although historians always ask questions as they read (see 3a for advice on active reading) and a thesis statement arises from the historian's attempt to answer a question, a question is not, in itself, a thesis. "Why were Mohandas Gandhi's methods successful in the movement to achieve India's independence from Great Britain?" is a valid historical question, but it is *not* a thesis statement.

- **A thesis is *not* a statement of fact.** While historians deal in factual information about the past, a fact, however interesting, is simply a piece of data. The statement "Mohandas Gandhi led the movement for India's independence from Britain" is *not* a thesis.

- **A thesis is *not* a statement of opinion.** Although a thesis statement must reflect what you have concluded, it cannot be a simple statement of belief or preference. The assertion "Mohandas Gandhi is my favorite political leader of the twentieth century" does *not* constitute a thesis.

In short, a thesis is *not* a description of your paper topic, a question, a statement of fact, or a statement of opinion, although it is sometimes confused with all of the above. Rather, a thesis is *a statement that reflects what you have concluded about the topic of your paper, based on a critical analysis and interpretation of the source materials you have examined.*

For the assignment given above, the following sentence *is* an acceptable thesis.

Mohandas Gandhi's decision to respond to force with acts of civil disobedience focused the world's attention on the legitimacy of British rule of India; his indictment of British colonial policy in the court of public opinion did far more damage to the British military than any weapon could.

You should note three things about this statement.

- First, while the thesis is not itself a question, it *is* an **answer to a question**—in this case, the question posed above: "Why were Mohandas Gandhi's methods successful in the movement to achieve India's independence from Great Britain?" A thesis usually arises from the questions you pose of the text or texts as you engage in active reading.

- Second, the thesis is **specific**. In attempting to answer the historical question raised above, the writer did not make a broad generalization like "Gandhi was successful because people thought he was a good person" or "Gandhi succeeded because the British were treating the Indians badly." Rather, the thesis makes a specific claim: that the contrast between Gandhi's use of civil disobedience and the use of force by the British had a significant impact on public opinion.

- Third, a thesis is always a **debatable** point, a *conclusion* with which a thoughtful reader might disagree. In other words, **the thesis makes an assertion or a claim that sets up an *argument***. It is the writer's job, in the body of a paper, to provide an argument based on evidence that shows his or her reasons for reaching a particular conclusion and that will convince the reader that his or her thesis is a valid one.

The thesis, then, is the heart of your paper. It presents what you have concluded about the topic under discussion and provides the focal point for the rest of the essay.

To ensure that your thesis really is a thesis, review the Tips for Writers box on page 59.

4d Constructing an argument

One reason you might find it difficult to develop a thesis statement is that you feel hesitant to come to independent conclusions about the meaning and significance of the materials you are working with. After all, what if your interpretation is wrong? It often seems safer just to reiterate the topic, or ask a question, or state a fact with which no one could argue. But, as noted in 4c, to write an effective history paper, you must be willing to reach a conclusion about your subject that could be challenged or debated by an intelligent reader. While this may seem intimidating, keep in mind that historical issues are

Tips for Writers
Testing Your Thesis

If . . .		Then . . .
Your proposed thesis does no more than repeat the topic you are writing about	→	It is *not* a thesis.
Your proposed thesis poses a question without suggesting an answer	→	It is *not* a thesis.
Your proposed thesis merely articulates a fact or series of facts	→	It is *not* a thesis.
Your proposed thesis simply reflects a personal belief or preference	→	It is *not* a thesis.
BUT		
If . . .		**Then . . .**
Your proposed thesis • suggests an answer to a question you have posed as a result of your reading, *and* • is specific, rather than general, *and* • is debatable (that is, it asserts a conclusion with which a reader might disagree), *and* • can be supported by evidence from the sources	→	It *is* a thesis.

seldom clear-cut and that professional historians, working from the same sources, often disagree with one another or form different interpretations. It is unlikely that there is only one correct point of view concerning the topic you have been assigned or only one correct interpretation of the sources you are examining. You do not need to convince your readers that your thesis or argument represents the *only* possible interpretation of the evidence. You do, however, need to convince them that your interpretation is valid. You will be able to do this only if you have provided concrete evidence from reliable sources in support of your argument and have responded honestly to opposing positions.

4d-1   Supporting your thesis

To support your argument, you must offer evidence from your sources. Imagine that you have been given the following assignment in a course on the history of science: "Analyze the role played by experiment and observation in William Harvey's *On the Motion of the Heart and Blood in Animals*." As you begin to analyze the text, you notice that Harvey describes his experimental method and his observations in great detail. You also notice, however, that Harvey drew inspiration from the analogy he saw between the sun as the center of the solar system and the heart as the center of the body, and that this analogy led him to consider whether the blood, like the planets, might move about the body in a circular motion. Your thesis will depend on the conclusion you reach, after careful and active reading of the text, about which of these elements was more significant in Harvey's discovery of circulation. If you conclude that experimentation and observation were more important in Harvey's thinking, your thesis statement might look like this:

> Although Harvey sometimes used analogies and symbols in his discussion of the movement of the heart and the blood, it was his careful observations, his elegantly designed experiments, and his meticulous measurements that led him to discover circulation.

If, however, you conclude that Harvey's philosophical commitments were more significant, you might write the following.

> Harvey's commitment to observation and experiment mark him as one of the fathers of the modern scientific method; however, a careful reading of *On the Motion of the Heart and Blood in Animals* suggests that the idea of circulation did not arise simply from the scientific elements of his thinking, but was inspired by his immersion in neo-Platonic philosophy.

Note that you could come to *either* of these conclusions after a careful examination of the text. What is essential is that you support your thesis by constructing an argument with evidence taken from the text itself. It is *not* enough simply to make a claim and expect readers to agree. In the first instance, you would support your thesis by pointing to examples of experiments Harvey designed and carried out. You might also note Harvey's emphasis on quantification and the care with which he described experiments that could be replicated. In the second instance, you might note the number of times Harvey compares the heart to the sun, thus providing an analogy for circulation. You might also note that Harvey was unable to observe circulation directly, since capillaries are too small to be seen without a microscope, which was not available at the time, and that his belief in circulation therefore required an intuitive leap that could not have been drawn solely from observation. In both cases, you would need to cite *specific* instances from the text to support your thesis, integrating quotations from the source as appropriate. (For more on using quotations, see 7a-2.)

4d-2 Responding to counterevidence and anticipating opposing viewpoints

Acknowledging counterevidence—source data that does not support your argument—will not weaken your paper. On the contrary, if you address counterevidence effectively, you strengthen your argument by showing why it is legitimate despite information that seems to contradict it. If, in the example above, you wanted to argue for the primacy of experiment and observation in Harvey's work, you would need to show that these elements were more significant than his interest in philosophical speculation. If you wanted to argue that his philosophy was more important, you would have to demonstrate that it was his keen interest in the ways in which some philosophers interpreted the centrality of the sun in the universe as a metaphor that allowed him to interpret what he observed about the motion of the blood and the heart in creative new ways. In either case, your argument would need to be based on a consideration of the evidence and counterevidence contained in the relevant source or sources, not merely on your own gut feelings.

Similarly, if you are writing an essay in which you are examining secondary sources, you should demonstrate that you are aware of the work of historians whose interpretations differ from your own; never simply ignore an argument that does not support your interpretation. It is perfectly legitimate to disagree with others' interpretations; this is, after all, one of the purposes of writing a book review or a historiographic essay (see 3d-1 and 3d-2). In disagreeing, however, you need to treat opposing viewpoints with respect; you should never resort to name-calling, oversimplifying, or otherwise distorting opposing points of view. *Your essay will be stronger, not weaker, if you understand opposing arguments and respond to them fairly.*

A good argument, then, does not ignore evidence or arguments that seem to contradict or weaken the thesis. If you discover information that does not support your thesis, do not suppress it. It is important to acknowledge *all* of your data. Try to explain to readers why your interpretation is valid, despite the existence of counterevidence or alternative arguments, but do not imply that your interpretation is stronger than it is by eliminating data or falsifying information. Rather, a successful paper responds to counterevidence and differing interpretations by addressing them directly and explaining why, in your view, they do not negate your thesis.

Note: Of course, if the counterevidence is too strong, you will need to adjust, or even completely change, your thesis. Always be open to the possibility that your initial conclusions might need to be modified in response to the evidence you find. (For more on the process of gathering evidence and developing a working thesis, see Chapter 5.)

4e   Organizing your paper

Even after analyzing an assignment, reading the sources carefully with a historian's eyes, developing a thesis, and finding evidence in the sources that supports your thesis, you may still find it difficult to organize your ideas into an effective paper. History papers, like other academic writings, include an introduction, a body, and a conclusion. This section examines the specific elements that your history instructor will expect to find in each of these parts of your paper.

4e-1   Drafting an introduction

The introductory paragraph of your paper is in many ways the most important one and therefore the most difficult to write. In your introduction, you must (1) let your readers know what your paper is about and provide background information on the texts, people, or problems under discussion; (2) put the topic of your paper into context; and (3) state your thesis. You must also attract your readers' attention and interest. The opening paragraph, then, has to frame the rest of the paper and make readers want to continue reading. There is no magic formula for writing an effective first paragraph. You should, however, keep the following conventions in mind.

Do not open with a global statement. Unsure of how to start, many students begin their papers with phrases like "Throughout history . . ." or "From the beginning of time . . ." or "People have always wondered about . . ." You should avoid generalizations like these. First, you cannot prove that they are true: How do you know what people have always thought or done? Second, these statements are so broad that they are virtually meaningless; they offer no specific points or details to interest readers. Finally, such statements are so vague that they give readers no clue about the subject of your paper. It is much more effective to begin with material specific to your topic.

The following opening sentence comes from the first draft of a student paper on William Harvey's *On the Motion of the Heart and Blood in Animals.*

INEFFECTIVE

From ancient times, people have always been interested in the human body and how it works.

Although there is nothing grammatically wrong with this sentence, it is not a particularly effective opening. For one thing, it is such a general statement that readers will be inclined to ask, "So what?" In addition, it gives readers no indication of what the paper is about. Will the essay examine ancient Greek medical theory? Chinese acupuncture? Sex education in twentieth-century American schools?

In revising the sentence, the student eliminated the general statement altogether and began instead with a description of the intellectual context of Harvey's work.

EFFECTIVE

For the scholars and physicians of seventeenth-century Europe, observation and experimentation began to replace authoritative texts as the most important source of information about human anatomy and physiology.

From this one sentence, readers learn four things about the subject of the paper: the time frame of the discussion (the seventeenth century), the place (Europe), the people involved (scholars and physicians), and the topic (the importance of experiment and observation in the biological sciences). Readers' curiosity is also piqued by the questions the sentence implies: Why did experimentation begin to replace authoritative texts? Was this change a subject of controversy? Who was involved? How did this change in method affect the science of biology and the practice of medicine? In other words, this opening sentence makes readers want to continue reading; they want to know the author's thesis.

Include your thesis in the first paragraph.   If your opening sentence has been effective, it will make your readers want to know the main point of your paper, which you will state in the thesis. As you read works by professional historians, you may notice that the introduction to a journal article or a book may be long, even several paragraphs, and the author's thesis may appear anywhere within it. Until you become skilled in writing about history, however, it is best to keep your introduction short and to state your thesis in the first paragraph. The following is the first draft of the introductory paragraph for the paper on Harvey.

INEFFECTIVE

From ancient times, people have always been interested in the human body and how it works. William Harvey was a seventeenth-century physician who performed many experiments and discovered the circulation of the blood.

This introduction begins with the ineffective opening sentence we looked at above. The "thesis statement" that follows is not really a thesis at all; it is simply a statement of fact. (For more on writing an effective thesis, see 4c.) Moreover, no clear connection is established between the ideas contained in the opening sentence and Harvey. From this first paragraph, a reader would have no idea what the paper was about, what its central point might be, or what to expect in the pages that follow.

In the final version of this introductory paragraph, the student uses the revised opening sentence and incorporates a more effective thesis, which is underlined here.

EFFECTIVE

For the scholars and physicians of seventeenth-century Europe, observations and experimentation began to replace authoritative texts as
the most important source of information about human anatomy and
physiology. This trend is clearly illustrated in the work of William
Harvey, who designed controlled experiments to measure blood flow.
However, <u>Harvey was not led to his revolutionary discovery of the circulation of the blood by experimentation alone; he was also inspired
by flashes of intuition and philosophical speculation</u>.

In this introductory paragraph, the connection between
Harvey and the rise of observation and experiment in the
seventeenth century is clear. Moreover, the thesis statement reflects the author's conclusions and anticipates
the argument that will follow; we can expect that in the
course of the paper, the author will support his or her
argument by discussing Harvey's experimental method,
his philosophical speculations, his moments of intuition, and the role all three played in his theories about
circulation.

Plan to rewrite your opening paragraph.   Because the opening paragraph plays such a crucial role in the overall
effectiveness of your paper, you should always plan on
revising it several times. In addition, when the paper is
complete, be sure to check each section against the introduction. Does each paragraph provide evidence for your
thesis? Is it clear to your reader how each point relates
to the topic you have established in your introduction?
Knowing that you will have to rewrite your introduction
can be reassuring if you are having trouble beginning
your paper. Write a rough, temporary opening paragraph,
and return to it when you finish your first draft of the
entire paper. The act of writing your draft will help you
clarify your ideas, your topic, and your thesis.

4e-2 Writing clear and connected paragraphs

In your introduction, you present your subject and state
your thesis. In the body of your paper, you provide an
argument for your thesis based on evidence from the
sources you have been reading and answer any objec-
tions that could be raised. The organization of your paper
will be driven by the evidence that supports your thesis.

You should think of each paragraph as a building block in your argument that presents one specific point. If the point of each paragraph is not clear, or if its relationship to the thesis is vague, the reader will not be able to follow your reasoning, and your paper will be weak and unconvincing. (For more on constructing an argument, see 4d.) The following advice will help you write well-organized, cohesive, and persuasive paragraphs.

Begin each paragraph with a topic sentence.   Each paragraph should have one driving idea that provides support for your paper's overall thesis. This idea is usually asserted in the *topic sentence*. If you have made an outline, your topic sentences will be drawn from your list of the main points you wish to cover in your paper. (For advice on making an outline, see 5f.)

Provide support for the paragraph's main point.   Each subsequent sentence in the paragraph should provide *evidence* in the form of examples, quotations from the text(s), or statistics that support the main point of the paragraph as stated in the topic sentence. Make sure that you do not wander off the point. If you include irrelevant information, you will lose momentum, and your readers will lose the thread of your argument. Instead, make sure you choose examples that provide clear and sufficient support for your main point. If you are using a direct quotation as evidence, make sure you explain to the reader why you are including this quotation by integrating it grammatically into your text and framing it in a way that shows how it supports your point. (For more information on how and when to quote, see 7a.)

Make clear connections between ideas.   To be convincing, your evidence must be clear and well organized; the sentences in each paragraph must follow one another in a logical fashion. Transitional words and phrases tell your readers how the individual sentences in your paragraph are connected to each other. To choose transitions that are appropriate, you need to think about how your ideas are related. The following are some transitional words and phrases that indicate particular kinds of relationships.

- **To compare:** *also, similarly, likewise.*
- **To contrast:** *on the one hand/on the other hand, although, conversely, nevertheless, despite, on the*

contrary, still, yet, regardless, nonetheless, notwith-standing, whereas, however, in spite of.
- **To add or intensify:** *also, in addition, moreover, further, too, besides, and.*
- **To show sequence:** *first* (and any other ordinal number), *last, next, finally, subsequently, later, ultimately.*
- **To indicate an example:** *for example, for instance, specifically.*
- **To indicate cause-and-effect relationships:** *consequently, as a result, because, accordingly, thus, since, therefore, so.*

Writing paragraphs: an example. The following is a paragraph from the first draft of a paper on Chinese relationships with foreigners during the Ming period.

INEFFECTIVE

The Chinese were willing to trade with barbarians. They distrusted foreigners. Jesuit missionaries were able to establish contacts in China. During the seventeenth century, they acquired the patronage of important officials. They were the emperor's advisers. Chinese women bound their feet, a practice that many Europeans disliked. Relations between China and Europe deteriorated in the eighteenth century. The Jesuits were willing to accommodate themselves to Chinese culture. Chinese culture was of great interest to the scholars of Enlightenment Europe. Matteo Ricci learned about Chinese culture and became fluent in Mandarin. He adopted the robes of a Chinese scholar. He thought that Christianity was compatible with Confucianism. The Jesuit missionaries had scientific knowledge.

Although each sentence is grammatically correct, this paragraph as a whole is very confusing. In the first place, it has no clear topic sentence; readers have to guess what the writer's main point is. This confusion is compounded by unclear connections between ideas; the paragraph lacks transitional words or phrases that alert readers to the connections that the writer sees between ideas or events. The paragraph is also poorly organized; the writer seems to move at random from topic to topic.

The following is a revised version of the same paragraph.

EFFECTIVE

The Chinese of the Ming dynasty were deeply suspicious of foreigners; *nevertheless*, Jesuit missionaries were able to achieve positions of honor and trust in the imperial court, ultimately serving the emperor as scholars and advisers. *At first glance*, this phenomenon seems baffling; upon closer consideration, *however*, it becomes clear that the Jesuits' success was due to their willingness to accommodate themselves to Chinese culture. *For example*, one of the most successful of the early Jesuit missionaries, Matteo Ricci, steeped himself in Chinese culture *and* became fluent in Mandarin. To win the respect of the nobles, he *also* adopted the robes of a Chinese scholar. *Moreover*, he emphasized the similarities between Christianity and Chinese traditions. *Because* of their willingness to adapt to Chinese culture, Jesuit missionaries were accepted by the imperial court until the eighteenth century.

This paragraph has been improved in several ways. First, a **topic sentence** (which is underlined) has been added to the beginning. Readers no longer need to guess that this paragraph will address the apparent contrast between sixteenth-century Chinese suspicion of foreigners and the imperial court's acceptance of Jesuit missionaries.

Second, the author has clarified the connections between ideas by including **transitional words and phrases**. These transitions (which are italicized) illustrate several different kinds of relationships—including contrast, cause and effect, and sequence—and allow readers to follow the writer's argument.

Third, the paragraph has been reorganized so that the **relationships** between events are clearer. For example, the revised paragraph states explicitly that the Jesuits' adaptation to Chinese customs was the key reason for the success of European missionaries during the Ming dynasty; this connection is obscured in the original paragraph by poor organization.

Finally, the writer has removed references to foot binding and to European interest in China during the Enlightenment. Both are interesting but irrelevant in a paragraph that deals with Chinese attitudes toward Europeans.

4e-3 Writing an effective conclusion

Your paper should not come to an abrupt halt, yet you do not need to conclude by summarizing everything that you have said in the body of the text. An effective conclusion performs two vital functions. First, it brings the paper full circle by reminding the reader of the thesis and reiterating the *most important* points that were made in support of the thesis. Second, it answers the main question that your reader, having read the entire paper, will want to know: "Why is this important?" Thus, it is usually best to end your paper with a paragraph that states the most important conclusions you have reached about your subject and the reasons you think those conclusions are significant.

Note: A common pitfall for students is to end the paper with some new idea or fact. You should avoid introducing new ideas or information in the conclusion. If an idea or a fact is important to your argument, you should introduce and discuss it earlier; if it is not, leave it out altogether.

The following is the first draft of the conclusion for the paper on Christian missionaries in China.

INEFFECTIVE

The Jesuit missionaries were sent to China in the Ming period. Some had good relationships with the emperor, but others did not. Some learned Mandarin and dressed in court robes. The pope would not let the Chinese worship their ancestors, but some Jesuits thought that Confucianism and Christianity were compatible. Another interesting aspect of Chinese culture at the time was the practice of foot binding.

This conclusion is ineffective for several reasons. First, there are no verbal clues to indicate that this is, in fact, the conclusion. In addition, it is too general and vague: Which missionaries had good relationships with the emperor, and which did not? Moreover, although it lists some of the key elements of the paper, it fails to indicate how these ideas are connected. Most important, perhaps, this conclusion does not suggest why the various ideas presented in the paper are important; in other words, it fails to answer the questions "So what? Why is this important?" Finally, a new topic is introduced in the last sentence.

In the revised version of the conclusion, these problems have been addressed.

EFFECTIVE

Thus, if we look at the experience of the Jesuits in China, it seems that their success or failure depended largely on the degree to which they were able to adapt to Chinese culture. The most successful missionaries learned Mandarin, adopted Chinese court dress, and looked for parallels between Christianity and the teachings of Confucius. It was only when the Church became more conservative — forbidding Chinese Christians, for example, to venerate their ancestors — that the Christian missionary effort in China began to fail. Ultimately, willingness to accept traditional Chinese culture and practices may have been a better way to gain converts than preaching complicated sermons.

This conclusion has been improved in several ways: It includes key transitional words (*thus, ultimately*) that indicate that the writer is drawing conclusions. It reiterates the important elements of the paper's argument but leaves out information that is either very general ("the Jesuit missionaries were sent to China in the Ming period") or too vague ("some had good relationships with the emperor, but others did not"). Moreover, unlike the earlier version, it is explicit about how the key topics in the paper — the flexibility of the Jesuit missionaries in adapting to Chinese culture, the parallels the missionaries drew between Christianity and Confucianism, and the institution of more conservative policies — are related. It does not add any new topics, however interesting those topics might be. And, most important, this version, unlike the first draft, clearly outlines the significance of the conclusions that the writer has reached: the Jesuit experience in China tells us something about the relationship between culture and religious belief.

4f Revising for content and organization

One of the biggest mistakes you can make with any writing assignment is to leave yourself too little time to revise and edit your work. A paper written the night before it is due is never of the highest caliber and usually bears the hallmarks of careless writing: sloppy mistakes in reasoning, awkward constructions, poor word choice, and lack of clear organization. To write an effective history paper, you *must* allow yourself time to review your paper, preferably at least twice: once to revise it for content and organization, and once to edit it for sentence style and grammatical correctness. (For advice on editing for style and grammar, see 4g.)

The word *revise* comes from the Latin *revisere*, which means "to look at again." When you revise a paper, you are, quite literally, looking at the paper again with critical eyes. To begin revising your paper, you need to read it critically, as if it were someone else's work. (For advice on critical reading, see 3a.) You should read for logic and clarity, making sure that your evidence is sufficient and that it supports your thesis. Be ruthless: eliminate all extraneous material from the final draft, however interesting it may be. For instance, if you are writing about the role that Chinese laborers played in the westward expansion of the American railroads, do not spend three paragraphs discussing the construction of the steam locomotive. If your paper concerns the American government's treatment of Japanese citizens during World War II, do not digress into a discussion of naval tactics in the Pacific theater. You must be willing to rearrange the order of material, do additional research to support weak points in your argument, and even change your entire thesis, if necessary. Obviously, you need to allow plenty of time for this part of the writing process, which may involve several drafts of the paper. The questions in the following Tips for Writers box will help you revise the content of your own paper or write an effective peer review for a classmate.

Tips for Writers
Revising for Content and Organization

- Does the first paragraph introduce the subject of the paper and provide information about the texts, people, or problems under discussion?
- Does the paper have a real thesis that is *specific* and *debatable*? Is the thesis clearly stated in the first paragraph?
- Does the paper provide sufficient evidence to support the thesis? Has counterevidence been carefully considered and addressed?
- Is the paper's argument clear and logical? Has the evidence from sources been synthesized into a cohesive structure?
- Have historical subjects been treated with respect? Does the paper avoid generalizations, anachronisms, and bias in both its language and its assumptions?
- Does each paragraph address one specific point, stated clearly in a topic sentence, and does each point support the paper's central argument?

- Is each paragraph clearly and logically organized? Do transitional words and phrases signal relationships within and between paragraphs?
- Has any irrelevant or extraneous material been eliminated?
- Does the conclusion tie together the paper's ideas?
- Is the paper properly documented? (See 6b and Chapter 7.)

4g Editing for style and grammar

Once you have finished revising your paper for matters of content and organization (see 4f), you are ready for editing, the final stage of the writing process, in which you focus on sentence style and grammatical correctness.

Uncorrected grammatical errors, misspelled words, and typographical mistakes can all detract from the effectiveness of your paper. At best, they suggest a lack of care and seriousness on the part of the author. At worst, they may actually obscure your meaning and make your argument difficult to follow. It is always a good idea to present your work in a professional manner by proofreading and editing your final draft. The following suggestions will help ensure that your paper is ready to be submitted.

Check for typographical and spelling errors.   You can do this effectively only by reading your paper over slowly and carefully. While your computer may automatically correct some typing or spelling errors, it will not correct everything. Spell-check programs will help you avoid *some* mistakes, but they will not pick up words *spelled* correctly but *used* incorrectly or in the wrong context (for example, *Mink dynasty* instead of *Ming dynasty*). Use your spell-checker, but do not rely on it. You can find lists of commonly misspelled words both in print and online.

Correct grammatical mistakes.   In oral communication, body language, gestures, and tone of voice combine with language to convey your meaning. Your listeners can ask questions if they are confused, and you have the opportunity to restate, rephrase, or otherwise clarify your statements. In writing, however, you must rely solely on the written word. Here, grammar is your friend; while grammatical errors can obscure your meaning and confuse the reader, observing the rules for constructing sentences and using punctuation correctly will ensure clear communication between you and your audience. For this reason, attention to grammar and punctuation is crucial.

It is beyond the scope of this manual to cover the basic grammatical rules, but the tip box starting below will help you avoid a few of the most common grammatical errors.

Tips for Writers
Common Grammatical Errors (and How to Avoid Them)

Plurals and Possessives

Typically, a **plural** (indicating more than one) is made by adding an *s* or *es* to the end of a noun. A **possessive**, as the word suggests, indicates ownership. Because plurals and possessives sound the same, a listener has to determine which is meant from the context. In writing, a visual clue—an apostrophe (')—is used to indicate a possessive, according to the following rules:

- For most singular nouns, add *'s*:

  Without parliamentary consent, the king's options for increasing his revenue were limited.

  Columbus's account of his first voyage reflects his conviction that he had reached Asia.

- For plural nouns that end in an *s*, add an apostrophe:

  The soldiers' health deteriorated dramatically under the conditions of trench warfare.

- For plural nouns ending in a letter other than *s*, add *'s*:

  The origins of the Children's Crusade are rooted in medieval religious ideology.

Contractions

Apostrophes are also used to signify a **contraction**: a group of words shortened by omitting some letters. For example, *she is/she's*, *would have/would've*, and so forth. In formal writing, you should not use contractions. Make sure you expand contractions correctly. For example, when spoken, *should've* (should have) may sound like *should of*; do not let your ears deceive you.

Take a minute to memorize the following contractions that often trip up students; your professors will thank you.

- **It's** is a contraction for *it is*. **Its** (*without* the apostrophe) is the possessive of the word *it*.

  Incorrect: During the Middle Ages, ginger was valued for it's medicinal qualities.

  Correct: During the Middle Ages, ginger was valued for its medicinal qualities.

- Don't confuse **there** (indicating a place), **they're** (contraction for *they are*), and **their** (possessive form of *they*).

Sentence Fragments

A **sentence** is a group of words that conveys a complete thought. In contrast, a **sentence fragment**, as its name implies, *looks* like a sentence, but is really only a part of a sentence; it simply does not make sense on its own. A sentence fragment is created when a **dependent clause** is presented as a sentence, an easy mistake to make, since like a sentence, it contains a subject and a verb. However, *unlike* a sentence, a dependent clause cannot stand alone; taken out of its paragraph, it does not make sense because it does not contain a complete thought.

A sentence fragment is easy to fix, either by combining it with the sentence after or before it to create a complete thought or, in some cases, by eliminating the introductory word:

  Fragment: After the Panama Canal was built.

  Sentence: After the Panama Canal was built, it became possible to ship goods without sailing around South America.

  Fragment: Because the Mongols controlled the most extensive land empire in history.

  Sentence: The Mongols controlled the most extensive land empire in history.

Run-on Sentences

A run-on sentence looks like a single sentence but is really two sentences "glued together" without any punctuation or joined, incorrectly, by a comma.

  Incorrect: The Portuguese cultivated sugar cane in the Azores growing it was back-breaking work.

  Incorrect: The Portuguese cultivated sugar cane in the Azores, growing it was back-breaking work.

There are many ways to fix a run-on sentence, including:

- **Write two separate sentences:**

  The Portuguese cultivated sugar cane in the Azores. Growing it was back-breaking work.

- **Use a semicolon:**

  The Portuguese cultivated sugar cane in the Azores; growing it was back-breaking work.

- **Use a comma and a coordinating conjunction (*and, but, or, nor, for, so, yet*):**

  The Portuguese cultivated sugar cane in the Azores, but growing it was back-breaking work.

Using a variety of these sentence patterns will keep your writing interesting.

Numbers and Dates

- Use numerals when referring to specific dates or years:

  The Japanese bombed Pearl Harbor on December 7, 1941 [American style]; or The Japanese bombed Pearl Harbor on 7 December 1941 [Canadian and European style].

  The Black Death reached Europe in 1347.

- Use Roman numerals when referring to monarchs:

  Incorrect: Elizabeth 2 of England

  Correct: Elizabeth II of England

  Note that a monarch's name *as spoken* (Elizabeth the second of England) *does not* correspond with the correct *written* form (Elizabeth II of England).

- When referring to a century or decade, add an *s* without an apostrophe:

  Incorrect: The 1960's were characterized by upheaval.

  Correct: The 1960s were characterized by upheaval.

- Write out numbers that can be expressed in two or three words:

  Incorrect: the 17th century; 500 years ago

  Correct: the seventeenth century; five hundred years ago

  More complex numbers should be written in figures:

  1,586 bushels of wheat; $976.84.

Follow instructions about formatting.   Pay attention to any instructions you have been given about font, line spacing, margins, documentation format, and so forth. If no specific instructions have been provided, make sure you are consistent; do not switch font style or size, change the margins, or switch from footnotes to endnotes part way through the paper.

Additional online grammar resources.   Your campus writing center can provide helpful advice on all writing issues. There are also many excellent print and online resources that you can (and should) consult for more information; several of these are listed below.

- Grammar Bytes: Grammar Instruction with Attitude http://chompchomp.com/. Includes definitions of grammatical terms, handouts, and interactive exercises, and even a daily grammar exercise on Twitter.
- The Guide to Grammar and Writing, sponsored by the Capital Community College Foundation. http://grammar.ccc.commnet.edu/grammar/. Provides grammar instruction and interactive quizzes on the word, sentence, and paragraph levels, as well as advice on organizing and writing essays and research papers.
- Purdue University's Online Writing Lab (OWL) https://owl.english.purdue.edu/. Perhaps the most complete open-access writing and grammar guide. OWL contains worksheets that guide students through English grammar and sentence structure, as well as exercises they can use to test their knowledge. It also provides advice aimed at students for whom English is a second language (ESL). In addition, OWL provides general advice on the writing process, writing academic papers, and APA, MLA, and Chicago citation guides.
- University of Illinois at Urbana-Champaign, *Grammar Handbook,* http://www.cws.illinois.edu /workshop/writers/. This site provides a clear introduction to the basic rules of English grammar, sentence structure, and usage, as well as resources for ESL students and citation guides. It does not, however, include exercises.
- And finally, just for fun, the lyrics to several of Schoolhouse Rock's Grammar Rocks songs can be found at http://www.schoolhouserock.tv /Grammar.html/.

While you must follow grammatical rules, you *do* have some flexibility when it comes to style, or the way in which you write (simple versus complex sentences, highly descriptive versus stark wording). How you express yourself and the words you choose are a reflection of your own style. Nevertheless, historians tend to follow certain conventions governing language, tense, and voice that you will want to keep in mind when you write and revise your history papers.

4g-1 Choosing appropriate language

Section 4b introduced you to some of the habits of mind that will help you think like a historian: you need to respect your subject, avoid generalization and anachronism, and be aware of your biases and assumptions. As you write and revise your paper, make sure that your writing demonstrates that you have adopted these good thinking practices.

Avoid value-laden words.   Historians, as noted earlier in this chapter (see 4b), attempt to understand the people of the past in their own contexts rather than judge them by the norms of the present. If you use value-laden words such as *backward, primitive, uncivilized*, and *superstitious*, you are implying that your own period, culture, and perceptions are superior to those of the past. Passing judgment on the people of the past does not help us understand *what* they believed, *why* they believed it, or the social and cultural *context* in which they formed their beliefs.

Avoid biased language.   Always take care to avoid words that are gender-biased or that have negative connotations for particular racial, ethnic, or religious groups. You should never use expressions that are clearly derogatory. In addition, you should be aware that many words that were once acceptable are now deemed inappropriate. For example, the use of masculine words to refer to both men and women, once a common practice, is now viewed as sexist by many. Use *humankind* or *people* rather than *mankind*, and do not use masculine pronouns when referring to people of both genders.

In an attempt to avoid sexist language, students sometimes make a grammatical error instead. For example, in trying to eliminate the masculine pronoun *his* in the sentence "Each individual reader should form *his* own opinion," a student may write, "Each individual reader should form *their* own opinion." The problem with this new version is that the pronoun *their* is plural, while the antecedent, *reader*, is singular. A grammatically correct revision is "Individual readers should form their own opinions." In this sentence, the antecedent (*readers*) and the pronoun (*their*) are both plural.

Note that you cannot always rely on the books you are reading to alert you to biased language. In older publications, you may encounter previously common terms such as *oriental* or *negro* to refer to people, but these words are generally no longer used. Today, the preferred word for people of Asian heritage is *Asian*; people of African descent are generally called *black* or (for US history) *African American*.

Note: You cannot correct the language of your sources. If you are quoting directly, you must use the exact wording of your source, including any racist or sexist language. If you are paraphrasing or summarizing a paragraph containing biased language, you might want to use unbiased language when it does not distort the sense of the source. Otherwise, put biased terms in quotation marks to indicate to your readers that the words are your source's and not yours.

Avoid conversational language, slang, and jargon.   Because history papers are usually formal, and because slang often sounds anachronistic, you should use formal language rather than conversational language in your writing. Words with double meanings should be used only in their conventional sense, and you should also avoid jargon, or specialized language, which can often obscure your meaning. Finally, as noted in Tips for Writers on page 73, contractions (such as *wasn't* for "was not" and *won't* for "will not") are generally too informal for use in a history paper; use the expanded form instead.

Make your language as clear and simple as possible.   If you hope to convince your readers that your thesis is valid, they have to be able to understand what you are trying to say. The following suggestions will help ensure that your writing does not include elements that obscure your meaning.

- **Use your thesaurus judiciously.** A thesaurus can be an excellent tool for increasing your vocabulary. However, you should avoid the temptation simply to substitute your original word with a more "impressive" or "sophisticated" one, since the new word might not mean exactly what you intended. When you use a thesaurus, always use a dictionary to make sure you know the precise meaning of the replacement word.

- **Use the simplest word that makes your meaning clear.** Using a four-syllable word when a single-syllable word will do may sound pretentious; using five words (such as *due to the fact that*) where you can use one (*because*) is often just wordy.

- **Be as precise as possible.** Labels such as *college graduates, the poor, the Maori*, and *Protestants* create the impression that all members of a group think and behave in *exactly* the same manner. In reality, groups are composed of individuals, each of whom is different and acts independently. Do not say "women" agitated for the vote when you mean "English suffragists."

- **Replace vague references with specifics.** The use of phrases such as *other factors, additional forces*, or *outside influences* leaves the reader without necessary information. What, exactly, are these factors, forces, or influences? Vague references often disguise writers' lack of information or clear thinking—writers may use phrases like *other factors* because they are not really sure what those factors are. Vague references not only obscure your meaning but also can undermine your credibility.

- **Make your sentences clear and concise.** Your writing will be more interesting if you use sentences of varying length; however, you should avoid overly long sentences with several dependent clauses. Your readers should not become so entangled in the sentence that they no longer remember what the subject was by the time they reach the verb! Try reading your sentences out loud; it is sometimes easier to hear sentences that are too long or confusing than to recognize them in print.

4g-2 Choosing the appropriate tense

The events that historians write about took place in the past; therefore, you should use the past tense when writing a history paper. Students are sometimes tempted to use the historical present tense for dramatic effect, as in this example from a student paper.

INEFFECTIVE

The battle rages all around him, but the squire is brave and acquits himself well. He defends his lord fearlessly and kills two of the enemy. As the fighting ends, he kneels before his lord on the battlefield, the bodies of the dead and dying all around him. His lord draws his sword and taps it against the squire's shoulders. The squire has proven his worth, and this is his reward; he is now a knight.

Using the present tense may be an effective device if you are writing fiction, but it is awkward in a history paper. First, readers might become confused about whether the events under discussion happened in the past or in the present, especially if the paper includes modern assessments of the issue. Second, use of the present tense makes it easy for the writer to fall prey to anachronism (see 4b). Perhaps more important, writing in the present tense sounds artificial; in normal conversation, we talk about events that happened in the past in the past tense. The same approach is also best for writing.

Do use the present tense, however, when discussing the contents of documents, artifacts, or works of art because these still exist. Note, for example, the appropriate use of past and present tenses in the following example.

EFFECTIVE

Columbus sailed across an "ocean sea" far greater than he initially imagined. The admiral's *Journal* tells us what Columbus thought he would find: a shorter expanse of water, peppered with hundreds of hospitable islands.

The events of the past are referred to in the past tense (*sailed, imagined, thought*), and the contents of the *Journal* are referred to in the present (*tells*).

Historians also use the present tense when they are referring to the work of other scholars. Note, for example, this sentence from the annotated bibliography entry in Chapter 3: "Fletcher . . . argues that . . . Christians and Muslims did not achieve any real measure of mutual understanding in the period under discussion."

4g-3 Using active voice

In the *active voice*, the subject of the sentence is the actor. In the *passive voice*, the subject of the sentence is the object of the action; a passive sentence often avoids naming an actor. In addition to making writing sound dull and unnecessarily wordy, the passive voice can lead to writing that is confusing, vague, and unassertive—characteristics that you will want to avoid in your history papers.

Prefer the active voice. As noted in Chapter 1, historians are like detectives; they try to answer questions like *Who? What? When? Where?* and *Why?* Using the passive voice can obscure this information. Consider the following excerpt from a student essay.

PASSIVE VOICE

In 1521, Tenochtitlán was invaded and the Aztecs were defeated.

Because he uses the passive voice here, the writer omits a vital piece of information: *Who* invaded Tenochtitlán and defeated the Aztecs?

In addition, the passive voice sometimes hides fuzzy thinking and allows writers to be vague about the connections between people, events, and ideas. Note what happens, for instance, when the writer of the previous example uses the active voice.

ACTIVE VOICE

In 1521, the Spanish conquistador Hernán Cortés and his army, supported by native allies like the Tlaxcalans, lay siege to the city of Tenochtitlán. Three months later, the hardships of the siege and the devastation caused by a smallpox epidemic forced the Aztec ruler, Cuauhtemoc, to surrender.

Because he is using the active voice here, the writer must identify the actors (Cortés, his army, and his native allies). Moreover, using the active voice also forces him to consider the complexity of the historical reality: the "invasion" of Tenochtitlán was really a three-month siege, and the defeat of the Aztecs was the result of the combined efforts of Cortés's army and native allies, the devastating effects of a long siege, and the impact of a new and virulent disease. Using the active voice thus requires the writer to provide more—and more specific—information.

In addition, the passive voice makes the writer sound hesitant. For example, the expression "it can be argued that" suggests that the writer is unwilling to take responsibility for his or her arguments. If your evidence leads you to a certain conclusion, state it clearly. Similarly, the expression "it has been argued that" can confuse readers: Who has made this argument? How many people have made this argument, and in what context? Readers must have this information to evaluate the argument. Moreover, use of the passive voice can result in plagiarism. If one or more authors have argued a particular point, you should identify them in the text and provide a citation.

Use the passive voice in special situations.   While historians almost always prefer the active voice, the passive voice is useful in some special circumstances. Consider the following description of the Holocaust (verbs in the passive voice have been italicized).

> Hitler engaged in the ruthless oppression and systematic murder of the Jewish people. In 1933, Jews *were forbidden* to hold public office; by 1935, they *were deprived* of citizenship. In all, over six million Jews *were killed* as part of Hitler's "final solution."

In this passage, the writer wants to draw the reader's attention to the recipients of the action—the six million Jews killed in the Holocaust. The people acted on are more important than the actor. The passive voice, which focuses attention on the victims, is therefore appropriate. The passive voice, then, can be effective, but it should be used only occasionally and for a specific reason.

4g-4 Knowing when to use the pronouns *I, me,* and *you*

Although you may occasionally see the pronouns *I, me,* and *you* in history books and journal articles, most professional historians use these pronouns sparingly, or not at all, and most history instructors prefer students avoid them whenever possible. However, a number of professors find their use not only acceptable but actually preferable to more labored constructions like "this evidence leads one to conclude that." Since the conventions governing the use of personal pronouns are in flux, it is best to consult your instructor about his or her preference. In any case, be consistent; if you use personal pronouns in the first paragraph ("My argument is based on the evidence of several primary sources"), do not switch to an impersonal construction in the second ("On the basis of the evidence, one might argue that . . .").

5

Writing a
Research Paper

Chapter 4 introduced you to the basic elements of writing a history essay: developing a thesis, using evidence to construct an argument, organizing your material effectively, and writing clearly. Like a short essay, a research paper usually takes the form of an argument in support of a thesis based on evidence from sources. It differs from a short essay, however, in several ways. First, a research paper is more substantial, usually at least fifteen pages and often much longer. More important, a research paper requires that you go beyond the assigned readings for the course and engage in a significant amount of independent work.

Your instructor might assign a specific research topic, or the choice might be left entirely up to you. Most often, you will be given some choice within a general subject area. The syllabus for a course with a research paper might, for example, include a statement like this in its list of course requirements:

> Research paper on any topic covered in the course, chosen in consultation with me. This paper should be 15–18 pages and is worth 40% of your final grade.

You may find such assignments intimidating and secretly yearn for an assigned subject; it often seems easier to write about a topic that holds no interest for you than to face the task of defining your own area of investigation. However, when you choose your own research topic, you are actually doing the same work that a professional historian does: conducting research in order to answer the questions *you* have posed about a subject that *you* find compelling or problematic and then writing a paper that allows *you* to enter into a conversation with other scholars who are interested in similar questions and problems. The research paper, then, is both challenging and exciting. It allows you, while still a student, to undertake original research and perhaps even discover something new. This level of engagement with the sources, rather than its length, is what truly distinguishes the research project from other writing assignments.

Writing a research paper is a complex activity; it does not proceed in a simple linear fashion, step-by-step. For the sake of clarity, this chapter divides the process of writing a research paper into the following stages: choosing a topic and focusing on a research question that you will answer in your paper, developing a research plan, conducting research, taking effective notes, developing a working thesis, writing an outline, and revising your paper. Keep in mind, however, that real research involves a constant interaction of thinking, reading, and writing, and that the processes outlined in these sections will intersect and overlap.

5a Moving from topic to research question

Deciding what topic to write about can seem overwhelming. Out of an apparently infinite range of possibilities, how do you choose? The process is more manageable if you break it down into its component parts: choosing a broad subject that interests you, narrowing your focus to a topic that you will be able to write about in the time and space allotted, deciding what you want to know about that topic, and, finally, formulating the research question you want to answer in your paper.

5a-1 Choosing a topic

Since a research paper represents a significant investment of time and effort, you will produce your best work if you choose a topic that can sustain your interest over the course of an entire semester.

Start with the texts assigned for your class and find a general area that appeals to you. This might be a relatively wide-ranging subject, like "slavery and the Civil War." Obviously, this is much too broad—you will not be able to write an effective essay on this subject within the length of a typical research paper—so you will need to narrow your focus. However, you will not know what problems, issues, and questions exist within the larger framework of the subject that interests you until you familiarize yourself with the research done by other scholars.

Narrowing a broad subject to a feasible topic for a research paper always begins with reading. You might start with a textbook or a general history or survey of the period. In addition, you might want to consult dictionaries, encyclopedias, and other general resources to get some background information about your subject. Such sources should never be your main sources of information for research papers at the college level; most professors will not accept encyclopedias or dictionaries as sources for research papers. However, at the beginning of your project, a reputable encyclopedia or a specialized dictionary can provide useful background to get you started.

You should also determine what sources are available to you, either in your own college or university library, through interlibrary or consortium loans, or on the internet. For example, you might decide that it would be interesting to examine the views of artisans during the French Revolution, but if you cannot obtain enough sources of information on this subject, this will not be a workable topic. Similarly, you should find out whether the sources for the topic in which you are interested are written in a language that you can read fluently. You might find that there are extensive collections of sources on artisans in revolutionary France—written in French. In this case, is your command of the language sufficient for the research you hope to pursue?

5a-2 Focusing on a research question

As you do your preliminary reading, you should be looking for a particular aspect of the topic that you want to explore further. For example, if your topic is "slavery and the Civil War," you might be particularly interested in the role of abolitionists in the war, in the events and ideas that led up to the Emancipation Proclamation, or perhaps in what slaves thought about the war. Then, having identified what you hope to learn, you should be able to state your topic as a *single question* that can be answered as a result of your research. Ultimately, the answer to your research question will take the form of a *thesis*, the main argument of your paper. (See 4c and 4d for more background on developing thesis statements. For more detail on the role of a working thesis in a research paper, see 5e.) The following tips will help you ask good research questions.

- **Avoid questions that elicit simple description.** Focusing on a question such as "What was the Compromise of 1850?" or "What happened during the Battle of Bull Run?" can result in a paper that is merely a list of facts or a narrative reporting "what happened next," neither of which is a satisfactory research paper.

- **Avoid yes/no questions.** Your research question should not be one that would generate a simple yes or no answer. Once you have answered the question "Did free blacks play a role in the Union army?" where would you go from there?

- **Avoid questions that are too broad.** You will not be able to answer the question "What role did freed slaves play in the Civil War?" in a twelve- to fifteen-page paper.

- **Avoid leading or rhetorical questions.** Don't make unwarranted assumptions or presume a particular answer. The question "Why were Northern states more racially integrated than Southern states in the 1800s?" presumes that the North was, in fact, more egalitarian than the South. Such a question might lead you to collect only evidence that supports your assumption while ignoring evidence to the contrary.

- **Avoid speculative questions.** The question "What would have happened if the South had won the Civil War?" might provoke some interesting speculations, but it is *not* a question that could be answered by historical research. Instead, ask questions that will allow you to develop an argument based on evidence.

Since your goal is to create a thesis—and a paper—that takes a stand on a particular issue, you should ask *a meaningful historical question that calls for analysis and interpretation, and that might elicit some debate*. You might, for instance, look at a particular Union regiment and try to answer the question "How did white Union officers' assumptions about race affect the way they treated black soldiers under their command?" Such a question would allow you to enter a scholarly debate by formulating your own research-based opinion.

5b Developing a research plan

Section 5a hinted at the effort you will need to put into gathering, reading, and evaluating texts as you move from selecting and narrowing your topic to developing a research question. Obviously, a research paper is a serious scholarly endeavor; it cannot be done effectively at the last minute. Some professors break the research process into phases for you. You might be asked to produce a written topic proposal, an annotated bibliography, an outline, and a rough draft of your paper as separate graded assignments. In this case, much of the time-management difficulties involved in producing a research paper will have been done for you. More often, you will need to develop a research plan for yourself.

In planning your research strategy, you should consider what information you will need at each stage of the process, what sources you will need to consult in order to acquire that information, where you can find those sources, and how much time you will need to allow for research. Your research plan should reflect the subject you have chosen. For example, if the subject about which you are writing is obscure, locating sources may take significantly more time than if you are researching a relatively well-known subject. In the first case, you would probably need to allocate more time to evaluating primary sources that have not been well studied, while in the second instance, you would need more time to read and evaluate what other scholars have said. In either case, you would need to allow enough time to find and gather the materials needed; develop a working bibliography; read, evaluate, and take notes on your sources; and formulate a working thesis.

It is always safest to anticipate problems in gathering your sources: other people may have borrowed the books you want; you may want to travel to other libraries to use their rare book or other specialized collections; or you may need to consult materials housed in archives. If you are interested in a topic for which your own library has only limited sources, you might be able to borrow books from other colleges and universities on interlibrary loan, but processing those loans requires time, so plan accordingly.

Gathering and managing sources

Once you have decided on a topic, you should begin to gather sources for your paper. A good research paper contains references to a variety of sources, so you will need to develop a strategy for finding useful sources; you will also need to find ways to keep track of and synthesize the material they contain. Section 5c contains in-depth advice on conducting research, but the following preliminary tips provide an overview of how to begin gathering and working with your sources efficiently and intelligently.

Identify both primary and secondary sources. For most research papers, you will need to consult primary sources (letters, diaries, original documents, and so on). You will also need to consult secondary sources to become familiar with the ways in which other historians have interpreted this material; indeed, reading secondary sources will often lead you to interesting and relevant primary sources. Your secondary sources should reflect a balance of materials. While books are valuable sources, you should not confine your research to books; important recent research is often found in scholarly journal articles. You can find a wide variety of both primary and secondary sources on the internet; however, for many projects, internet sources alone are not sufficient for a research paper. For example, the texts of some primary sources found online are taken from older editions or translations in the public domain, since such texts are not covered by copyright restrictions; however, you can often find a printed edition or translation that reflects more recent scholarship. Moreover, many primary and secondary sources are not yet available on the internet; students who rely solely on electronic media will miss many fundamental and indispensable sources. Usually, then, you should consult both electronic and print sources in your research. In any case, as you read, be sure to evaluate the usefulness and reliability of your sources, whether you find them in print or online, using the criteria set out in Chapter 2. Finally, as you begin to gather sources, always keep your research question in mind. If you allow yourself to be sidetracked by fascinating material that is not related to your research question, your paper will lose its focus, and you may have trouble making your deadline.

Use nonwritten materials where appropriate. Although much of the work you do in a history course will depend on the reading and interpretation of written sources, historians also use a wide variety of nonwritten sources in their work. The following types of nonwritten materials may be useful to you in researching and writing your paper.

- **Maps** are especially useful for explaining geographical relationships, such as the movements of troops during a battle or the changes in the national boundaries of a particular area over time. Maps also reflect the geographical knowledge of the time in which they were made and the world-view of the people who made them.

- **Graphs and charts** are useful for illustrating statistical information, such as rates of marriages, births, or deaths, and changes in per capita income over a period of time.

- **Works of art** such as paintings and sculptures can illustrate artistic schools and styles, aesthetic tastes, and the social, cultural, and political interests and concerns of artists and their patrons. Artistic works such as monuments, textiles, and ceramics also help us understand societies of the past, particularly those for which only limited or no written records exist.

- **Photographs, cartoons, and other illustrations** may provide evidence that supports or contradicts the written sources, or may provide a unique perspective on events.

- **Oral history sources**, available as video recordings, audio recordings, and transcriptions of interviews, can be useful for information about events that have occurred within living memory. For example, the American Folklife Center of the Library of Congress houses the Veterans History Project, which collects (in addition to artifacts such as letters, photographs, and diaries) audio and video recordings of interviews with veterans (and civilians involved in the war efforts) from World War I through the more recent conflicts in Afghanistan and Iraq (www.loc.gov/vets/about.html). If you consult oral histories as primary sources, you need to evaluate them as you would any other primary source. However, conducting such interviews yourself is a different and more complicated

matter. Historians have developed special methodologies for doing oral history research. The Oral
History Association (www.oralhistory.org) provides
standards and guidelines for scholars. Donald
Ritchie's *Doing Oral History: A Practical Guide* is
also a useful resource. Seek your professor's advice
before engaging in this type of research yourself.

- **Diagrams**—such as a cross section of the Great
  Pyramid, architectural plans for Cluny Abbey, or
  schematics of scientific instruments or machines—
  can help the reader understand how parts are
  related to a larger whole. (For information on how
  to evaluate nonwritten sources, see the Tips for
  Writers box on pp. 14–15.)

Keep a working bibliography.   As you gather sources for
your research, be sure to keep a working bibliography in
which you record complete bibliographic information for
every item you have examined. (See 7c-2 for a description
of the elements that constitute complete bibliographic
information.) Nothing is more frustrating than to discover that you are missing page references for a quotation
you want to use or an idea you need to cite. You should
also record complete bibliographical information for any
nonwritten sources you examine or cite. If you have not
written many academic papers, you may find it difficult
to remember all of the elements that should be included
in a bibliographic entry; therefore, while doing your
research, you may want to keep this guide handy or carry
an index card listing the information you need to record.
If you are working online, research tools such as EndNote
(www.endnote.com), RefWorks (www.refworks.com), and
Zotero (www.zotero.org) can help you record and format
bibliographic information as you work.

Note: Do not make generating a bibliography an end in
itself. You still need to read the books and articles you
have found! Your final bibliography should include only
the materials you have read and found useful in writing
your paper.

5c   Conducting research

In order to explore the possible answers to your research
question, you will need to identify and evaluate a substantial number of primary and secondary sources of various types. Moreover, once you have developed a working

thesis, you will need to conduct even more research to refine and test it. But how do you go about finding the sources you need to write an effective research paper? This section provides some suggestions for how to use print and electronic research tools to locate reliable sources from among the wealth of materials available to you.

5c-1 Consulting human resources

You might have so much experience with the internet that your first instinct is to begin a research project by going online. However, you will save a great deal of time and effort if you begin by consulting two very important human resources.

Begin by consulting your professor. Although a research paper may seem daunting to you, remember that your professor has had a great deal of experience in conducting research and writing papers and is intimately familiar with the research produced by other historians. Take advantage of office hours, course-based websites, and other forums for consulting your professor. He or she can point you in a number of potentially fruitful directions. Ask your professor to recommend books and articles on your topic, and use them at the outset of your research. Your professor can also direct you to the most important scholarly journals in the field you are researching. And, of course, always consult your professor if you have any questions about what kinds of sources are required or allowed. For example, you might want to ask which internet sources are acceptable and whether field research such as oral history is allowed or encouraged.

Consult a reference librarian. Reference librarians are invaluable resources who are too often overlooked. They can be helpful in tracking down important print and electronic journals, bibliographies, book reviews, and other research tools. Reference librarians can also teach you how to search your university's online catalog and how to use the databases to which your university subscribes.

5c-2 Using the library's online catalog

After consulting your professor and a research librarian, you should start your own search for sources in your university's library. In addition to the stacks (where books that circulate are housed) and a reference room (where you can find noncirculating encyclopedias, dictionaries, indexes, atlases, and other reference materials), university libraries have scholarly journals, microfilm or microfiche materials (such as back issues of newspapers), audiovisual collections, and, frequently, a rare book room. Many universities also have archives that you might want to use for special projects. Archives generally have their own catalog; otherwise, you can locate all of these resources by using your library's online catalog. Besides directing you to the resources available in the library itself, most university library home pages provide links to a variety of electronic sources, including databases, online journals, subscription-only services, bibliographic management tools, and e-books. Many also provide links to other college and university libraries.

Search the online catalog.   If your professor has recommended a specific book, searching by title or author is simple and efficient. You can then find other books of interest by browsing the shelves in the area where your book is housed, since books on the same topic are grouped together (you can virtually "browse" the shelves by clicking on the call number of a useful book). Also consult the bibliographies and notes of any useful books you find; these will lead you to other primary and secondary sources of interest.

   If you don't have a particular book in mind, you can conduct a subject or keyword search. Keep in mind, however, that a subject search reflects the formal Library of Congress subject listings, which may not always be obvious. It is usually best to try a keyword search, using as many keywords as you can think of that might lead you to materials on your topic. For example, you might look for materials on the medieval plague by entering *bubonic plague, Black Death,* and *Black Plague,* each of which would yield slightly different results. You can search the online catalog most effectively by conducting an advanced or guided keyword search that allows you to include or exclude specific terms in your search parameters. For example, if you wanted to examine the plague in continental Europe in the fourteenth century, you could limit your search to *Black Death* AND *14th century* NOT *England.* The online catalog will provide instructions for conducting a guided keyword search, and the time you invest in learning how to do this will make your search much more efficient.

Broaden your research base. Unless you attend a major research university, you might want to expand your search to other institutions' holdings. Often, your library's home page will include links to local colleges and universities whose catalogs you can also search online. If you find materials of interest, you can usually order them through interlibrary loan; increasingly, articles can be sent electronically to your library or even directly to your own e-mail address.

5c-3 Using print and electronic reference sources

As noted in 5a-1, encyclopedias, dictionaries, atlases, and the like are usually not acceptable as sources for a research paper; however, you may find it useful to consult a variety of print and electronic references at the beginning of your research to get a general sense of the topic. You will find print sources in your library's reference room. The library's home page will typically provide links to reliable online reference sources as well, some of which are available only by subscription. Sometimes these sources may be organized for you by subject. For example, your library may provide a research guide for history that lists links to electronic resources of interest to historians.

Note: Some free encyclopedias are available online, but they are not all equally reliable. As noted in 2b-3, the popular online encyclopedia *Wikipedia* is a public forum that typically allows any reader to add or edit entries. Consequently, the entries may be inaccurate or biased, and most instructors will not accept *Wikipedia* as a reference in your paper. Before you use an internet reference source, make sure you know who has written the entries and what organization sponsors the website. Better still, use the links on your library's home page to guide you to appropriate online reference sources.

5c-4 Locating primary sources

Primary sources are the essential materials with which historians work, and you will find them in both print and electronic formats.

Books. Book-length sources, such as chronicles, memoirs, novels, and treatises, are available in their original form (manuscripts or printed texts), in scholarly editions (which may include introductions, commentaries, and notes that explain the text), or, in the case of foreign-language texts, in translation. Many are also available as e-books; Project Gutenberg (www.gutenberg.org) and Google Books (http://books.google.com/ebooks) provide online access to thousands of books of interest to historians. For some research projects, you may want to look at a *facsimile*: an exact reproduction of a text as it appeared when it was first published. Facsimiles, like other books, are available in both print and electronic formats. For example, you can find digital facsimiles for more than 36,000 books, pamphlets, and broadsides published in America before 1800 in *Early American Imprints*. Early printed books, manuscripts, or other valuable or rare texts may be found in rare book collections, although you may need special permission to use these materials.

Documents.   Shorter documents, such as letters and speeches, are often available in print in edited document collections. Specialized primary source collections for virtually every historical period worldwide can also be found online. For example, the Internet History Sourcebooks Project (www.fordham.edu/halsall) provides public domain and copy-permitted texts in ancient, medieval, and modern history, with additional sourcebooks in specialized areas such as African, East Asian, Islamic, Jewish, and Women's history. The *Digital Collections* of the Library of Congress (www.loc.gov/library/libarch-digital .html) comprises a rich collection of photographs, letters, maps, and sound recordings. As noted above, facsimiles of a wide variety of documents, such as Charles Darwin's notebooks or Lincoln's Gettysburg Address, can also be found online. Government documents are typically available in both print and electronic formats. Current and archived newspapers from around the world are available online; archived newspapers and magazines may also be found on microfilm or microfiche in your university library. Finally, you may be able to examine original primary sources such as letters, diaries, or wills directly at an archive.

5c-5 Locating secondary sources: using print and electronic periodical databases

Secondary sources take the form of monographs—books about a particular historical subject—or articles in scholarly journals. You can easily find books by searching the library's online catalog for print editions and e-books or by consulting online resources like Google Books or Project Gutenberg, noted previously. Recently published journal articles represent the most scholarly and up-to-date work on a topic; moreover, they frequently contain an overview of the academic work on the subject and provide references to other important books and articles, making them extremely valuable resources for a history research paper. However, finding relevant journal articles can be a bit more problematic than finding books. To find the most relevant articles for your topic, you need to use both print and electronic bibliographies, indexes, and periodical databases.

Many library reference rooms contain comprehensive print indexes, such as *Humanities Index* (also available electronically), which list important secondary sources and are arranged by subject matter for ease of browsing. Print indexes contain all the bibliographic information you need to track down an article; some indexes, such as *Historical Abstracts*, also contain abstracts, which briefly summarize the contents of the articles listed. Most likely, your school library also subscribes to dozens of electronic databases, such as *Periodicals Index Online*, which you can access through a research gateway from your school's website (at some schools, access is restricted to library terminals only). Generally speaking, electronic databases are easier to search than print indexes, and in some cases they also provide access to the full text of the articles listed, which gives them a distinct advantage. The Tips for Writers box on page 96 lists some of the most useful electronic databases for history students and what each offers. Check with your school's reference librarian for the best place to begin searching for scholarly articles in your subject area.

Typically, you can search databases by author, title, publication, date or date range, and keyword. Most databases provide tutorials on how to conduct searches, and since each database is a bit different, it is worth your time to familiarize yourself with each database you use.

5c-6 Finding internet sources

Used with care and with a critical eye, the internet can be an invaluable supplement to your research, providing access to a wide variety of primary and secondary

Tips for Writers
Electronic Databases

Database name	Content	Full-text archives*	Dates
America: History and Life	Abstracts of journal articles and book reviews published throughout the world covering the history of the United States and Canada	Full-text version available through Ebsco	1964–present
Arts and Humanities Citation Index	Index to journal articles and reviews in the arts and humanities, including history	Links to full-text articles	1975–present
Ebsco Academic Search Complete	Abstracted and indexed articles in a wide variety of academic fields, including history	Some	1887–present
Historical Abstracts	Abstracts of articles pertaining to world history from 1450; excludes United States and Canada	Some	1954–present
Humanities Full Text	Full-text articles in the humanities, including history	Yes	1995–present
Humanities Index	Index to articles in the humanities, including history	Some	1974–present
Journal Storage Project (JSTOR)	Abstract and full-text articles from scholarly journals dating back to the 1600s	Yes	1600s–within last 5 years
Project Muse	Articles in the humanities and social sciences	Yes	Date online to present
Social Sciences Citation Index	Social sciences, including history; this index is part of the *Web of Knowledge*	Some	1956–present

*Note: In many cases, databases will attempt to provide a link to the full text of an article, even if the article isn't included in the database's own archives. Check with your reference librarian to find out what is available.

sources that would otherwise be unavailable. As you move outside your library's electronic environment onto the internet, however, make sure to use caution. Be aware that many websites are useless for serious research; in fact, some instructors require that you consult them before using *.com* or *.org* sites in a paper. The following advice will help keep your internet search on the right track.

Begin by browsing links related to your topic from a source that you can trust. Your instructor may have useful links posted on his or her website, and your school library may keep an updated collection of links organized by discipline. In addition, if you come across a site that appears to be a reputable source on a particular topic, you may find that its links are also worth checking out.

In general, you will want to avoid doing simple keyword searches on search engines such as Bing and Google because the results will be overwhelming and the reliability of the links will be dubious. You can refine your search by using advanced search features to limit your search results to only education (.edu) or government (.gov) sites or to retrieve only those sites that have been recently updated. A good strategy for conducting an internet search is to use Google Scholar, which searches only academic sources, and then further refine your search by using the Advanced Scholar Search feature, which allows you to search by keywords, author, publication, date, and subject area. When you find a useful source that you might want to access again later, bookmark it or, if you are working from a public computer, e-mail yourself a link or jot down the URL.

As with a search of your library's online catalog (see 5c-2), use a variety of keywords in your initial search and be as specific as possible. For example, searching *Henry IV* will turn up websites on Henry IV of France, Henry IV of England, and Shakespeare's plays. You can narrow your search by using the advanced search feature or by using plus (+) or minus (–) signs *immediately before* the term to add or exclude specific search terms. For example, *Henry IV +England –Shakespeare* should yield only sites about King Henry IV of England.

Note: Always evaluate the reliability of any web site you plan to use by following the criteria outlined in 2b-3.

5c-7 Distinguishing among electronic sources

Since many types of sources can be accessed electronically, you may sometimes find yourself wondering where exactly your source has come from and how reliable it is. Is it from an electronic database? An online journal? A government website? When trying to make these important distinctions, keep the following points in mind.

Databases. Databases store digitized versions of materials that usually have print equivalents. (Some databases that are particularly useful for history students are listed in the Tips for Writers box on p. 96.) Although a database may contain a wide variety of sources, including popular titles, you can usually tailor your search to include only scholarly sources such as academic journals. In most cases, you will need to identify yourself as a student to access these resources. Note that the database will look like any other website, usually with a *.com* extension, but you won't see any advertisements or links to external sites.

Websites for periodicals. Many print periodicals—popular magazines, newspapers, and so forth—maintain companion websites. These websites are primarily for advertising and subscription purposes, and they are of limited use to researchers. You will likely be able to access the current edition and perhaps some of the more recent articles, but you will probably not be able to download older full-text articles without paying a fee.

Online-only journals have no print counterparts. To determine whether an online-only publication is credible—whether it is affiliated with an academic institution and if the articles are peer-reviewed—you should always check the "About" link.

Broadcast news websites. Most major news outlets—NBC, Fox, NPR, CNN—have websites that archive their news stories. In addition, some websites, like Yahoo! News, provide news in an Internet-only format.

Government websites. Government agencies typically provide useful information online for public use, including census and immigration data, legislative records, economic statistics, and historical documents. The URLs for these sites typically contain the extension *.gov* or, for state governments, *.us* plus a state abbreviation such as *.ma*.

Other websites. Countless organizations, schools, museums, foundations, and so on have websites to store and display their collections, which are of tremendous value to researchers. Websites from sources other than these (and the ones listed above), however, are probably either commercial—existing primarily to sell a product or collect advertising revenue—or personal. Commercial and personal sites are the two most unreliable types of online sources because they are generally biased and/or not scholarly. In general, avoid commercial or personal sites; if you do wish to use them, you should ask your instructor first and take extra precautions when evaluating them (see 2b-3).

5d Taking effective research notes

Your final paper will be only as good as the notes you take. There is no right or wrong way to take notes for a research paper. Many writers favor index cards that can easily be arranged and rearranged. Others prefer to use notebooks or legal pads. Still others type notes directly into an electronic file. Whatever method you use, the following techniques will make your note taking more effective.

Write as you read. As explained in 3a, reading and writing are interactive processes. The writing you do while reading can take many different forms. If you own some of the books you are using for your paper, or if you have made photocopies of some of the important materials you will be using, you might want to write directly on the text, underlining important points and making comments in the margins. Develop your own code for marginal notation so that you will be able to identify arguments that you find questionable, insights that you find important, or words that you need to define. (For further suggestions on writing as you read, see the Tips for Writers box on p. 30.) Another useful technique is to keep a research journal in which you keep notes on your sources as you read; note references for additional sources you want to consult; jot down any ideas, insights, or questions that occur to you; and record full bibliographic information about the sources you have consulted. This writing will help you clarify your thoughts about what you are reading and provide direction for your research.

Always record complete bibliographic information for your sources.
It is absolutely essential that you be able to identify the
source of any facts, ideas, visuals, or quotations that you
derive from your research, and that you clearly differen-
tiate the ideas of others from your own. Careful note taking will save you lots of time tracking down quotations
and will ensure that you do not plagiarize inadvertently.
(See Chapter 6.)

Take most of your notes in the form of summaries.   If you take
notes word for word from your source, you are simply
acting as a human photocopier. Your goal should be to
digest the information presented in your sources and
make it your own. It is much more useful to read carefully
and thoughtfully, *close the book*, and summarize *in your
own words* the section you have read. Then compare your
summary with the original, noting any important points
that you missed or anything that you misunderstood. At
this point, you should also check carefully to make sure
that you have not inadvertently taken any phrases or sentences directly from the original text. This type of note
taking will not only ensure that you really understand
the material but also help you avoid plagiarism.

Copy quotations accurately.   If you do decide to quote
directly from a source, make sure you copy the words
and punctuation exactly, and always use quotation marks
so that you will know it is a direct quotation when you
return to your notes. Do not try to improve the wording
of the original or correct the spelling or grammar. You
may, however, alert your readers to an error in spelling or
grammar by recording the error as it appears in the source
and then noting the mistake by adding the Latin word *sic*
(meaning "thus") in brackets: "Do not correct mispelled
[*sic*] words." (For advice on using and citing quotations,
see Chapter 7.)

5e   Developing a working thesis

As noted at the beginning of this chapter, writing a
research paper does not proceed in a simple, step-by-
step fashion. In reality, you won't finish conducting your
research and then begin to write; instead, the research
process looks more like Figure 5.1.

As Figure 5.1 suggests, thinking, reading, and writing are interactive processes. Once you have settled on

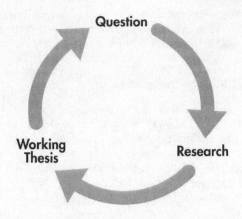

Figure 5.1   The Research Process

a research question, you begin to conduct research by identifying, locating, and reading primary and secondary sources that will help you answer that question. All this reading and the writing that attends it (listing questions, taking notes, jotting down ideas, and so on) are intended to stimulate and clarify your thinking. The result of all this thinking, reading, and writing is the generation of a *working thesis*: a single sentence in which you suggest a *tentative* answer to your research question.

A thesis, as noted in Chapter 4, is a statement that reflects what you have concluded about your topic based on a careful analysis and interpretation of the sources you have examined. (See 4c for details on how to write an effective thesis.) At this stage in the production of a research paper, however, your thesis is only a *working* thesis. This is because your research to this point has probably yielded some counterevidence — information that does not neatly support your thesis and that you must confront honestly. In other words, the evidence you uncover must always lead you to test your thesis: Does it still hold up as you discover new information or encounter new interpretations? Over the course of your research project, your working thesis will direct your ongoing research, and that continued research will, in turn, cause your thesis to evolve. As you continue to gather, read, and evaluate texts, organize your notes, and develop ideas about your topic, it is important to remain flexible. Willingness to modify a working thesis in response to research is the hallmark of a good historian.

5f Making an outline

Note taking, however precise and clear, is not an end in itself. The notes you take should be directed toward providing the information you will need to refine and support your working thesis as you attempt to answer your research question. If you have taken careful notes while conducting research, you will be able to organize them into an outline in which you sketch out the body of your paper.

The most important function of an outline is to provide a guide that identifies (1) the points you wish to cover and (2) the order in which you plan to cover them. A good outline will help you present the evidence that supports your thesis as a convincing argument. Some students have been trained to write formal outlines with roman numerals and various subheadings. If this method works for you, by all means use it. Many students, however, find formal outlines too constraining and prefer instead to write a less formal outline.

You might begin an informal outline by writing down the main points you want to discuss. These will form the *topic sentences* of paragraphs. Underneath each main point, list the *evidence* that supports it. Outlining your paper in this way has several advantages: it will reveal any points that require additional evidence; it will also help ensure that your evidence is organized logically and that each idea is connected to the ideas that precede and follow it.

Finally, remember that an outline is a tool. As you continue to think and write about your subject, you may discover new material or change your mind about the significance of the material you have examined. You may even change your thesis (which is why your thesis at this stage is still a working thesis rather than a final one). When this happens, you must be willing to revise your outline too; your outline, like your thesis, should evolve over the course of your research project. Ultimately, if you have taken careful and thorough notes and organized them effectively in an outline, what originally seemed to be a daunting task will become much more manageable.

The advice in Chapter 4 on following the conventions of writing history papers will then provide guidance as you write the first draft of your research paper.

5g Revising and editing your paper

As you revise, think about whether you have organized your argument in the most effective manner. Also determine whether you have presented enough evidence to support your thesis. You may even decide at this stage that you need to conduct additional research; this is one way in which revising a research paper differs from revising a short essay. Most important, you should reexamine your thesis in light of the evidence you have provided, evaluate the validity of that thesis, and modify or change it completely if necessary. (For more advice on revising your paper, see 4f.) Finally, once your revision is complete, you will need to edit your paper to correct grammatical and typographical errors. (See 4g for additional advice on word choice and grammar.)

A research paper is a complex project. It is unrealistic to expect that one or two drafts will be sufficient to do justice to it. As you plan your research, make sure you leave yourself sufficient time to revise and edit thoroughly. Obviously, a research paper represents a significant commitment of time, effort, and intellect. Nonetheless, the rewards are equally great, for it is in the research paper that you can experience the pleasures of truly original interpretation and discovery.

6
Plagiarism

WHAT IT IS AND HOW TO AVOID IT

Plagiarism is the act of taking the words, ideas, or research of another person and putting them forward without citation as if they were your own. It is intellectual theft and a clear violation of the code of ethics and behavior that most academic institutions have established to regulate the scholastic conduct of their members. Most colleges and universities have their own policies that define plagiarism and establish guidelines for dealing with plagiarism cases and punishing offenders, but the penalties for plagiarism are usually severe, ranging from an automatic F in the course to temporary suspension or even permanent expulsion from the school. Plagiarism, in short, is considered a very serious academic offense.

If we look simply at the dictionary definition, it would seem that acts of plagiarism are readily identifiable. And, indeed, some instances of plagiarism are obvious: deliberately copying lengthy passages from a book or journal article, submitting an essay written by a classmate as your own, or purchasing or downloading whole papers and submitting them under your own name. However, although some students unfortunately make a conscious decision to plagiarize, many more do so inadvertently. The reason is that, unlike the instances cited above, some situations in which you might use the words or ideas of another may seem murkier. Because of its seriousness, it is essential that you know exactly what kinds of acts constitute plagiarism. This chapter clarifies the concept and gives you some advice on how to avoid plagiarism.

6a What is plagiarism?

Read the following scenarios. Which of these would be considered plagiarism?

- A student borrows a friend's essay to get some ideas for his own paper. With his friend's permission, he copies portions of her essay, taking care, however, to cite all the sources she included in the original.

- A student finds useful information on a website that is not under copyright. She downloads and incorporates sections of this website into her paper but does not cite it since it is in the public domain.

- A student derives some key ideas for his paper from a book. Since he does not quote anything directly from this book, he does not provide any footnotes. He does, however, include the book in his bibliography.

- A student modifies the original text of an article by changing some words, leaving out an example, and rearranging the order of the material. Since she is not using the exact words of the original, she does not include a footnote.

The answer is that *all four* of these scenarios illustrate examples of plagiarism. In the first instance, the issue is not whether the student has permission from his friend to use her work. As long as the student is submitting work done by another as his own, it is plagiarism. Citing the sources that his friend has used does not mitigate the charge of plagiarism. In the second example, the fact that the student has used material that is not protected by copyright is irrelevant. She is guilty of plagiarism because she has submitted the words of another as her own. The third instance illustrates that the definition of plagiarism encompasses the use not only of someone else's words but also of that person's ideas; you must always acknowledge the source of your ideas in a footnote or an endnote, even if you specifically include the source in your bibliography. Finally, in the fourth example, changing some of the words, reorganizing the material, or leaving out some phrases does not constitute a genuine paraphrase; moreover, even an effective paraphrase requires a footnote.

As a history student, you are part of a community of scholars; when you write history papers, you become part of the intellectual conversation of that community. The published words and ideas of other historians are there to be used—but as a matter of intellectual honesty, you are bound to acknowledge their contributions to your own thought.

6b   Avoiding plagiarism

Most unintentional plagiarism can be traced to three sources: confusion about when and how to cite sources, uncertainty about how to paraphrase, and carelessness in taking notes and downloading internet materials.

6b-1   Citing sources to avoid plagiarism

When you derive facts and ideas from other writers' work, you must cite the sources of your information. Most students are aware that they must cite the sources of direct quotations. However, students sometimes assume, erroneously, that direct quotations are the *only* things they need to cite. In fact, borrowing ideas from other writers without documenting them is a form of plagiarism every bit as serious as taking their words. Therefore, you must provide citations for *all* information derived from another source, *even if you have summarized or paraphrased the information*. Furthermore, you must also cite your sources when you use other writers' *interpretations* of a historical event or text. For example, in *In the Devil's Snare*, historian Mary Beth Norton argues that the Salem witchcraft trials of 1692 can be understood only within the context of the Second Indian War. If you find her argument convincing and discuss this connection in a paper on the Salem witch trials, you need to provide a citation acknowledging Norton as the source of this idea. In short, whenever you use information derived from another person's work, build on another writer's ideas, or adopt someone else's interpretation, you must acknowledge your source. This enables your readers to distinguish between your ideas and those of others.

The only exception is that you do not need to provide citations for information that is common knowledge. *Common knowledge* is generally defined as well-known facts that are found in multiple reference works and are not subject to debate. For example, you might have learned from a particular book that the Civil War spanned the years 1861 to 1865, but you do not have to cite the book when you include this fact in your paper. You could have obtained the time span of the Civil War from any number of sources because it is common knowledge. The more you read about your subject, the easier it will be for you to distinguish common knowledge from information that needs a citation. When in doubt, however, it is better to be safe and cite the source. (For additional information on quoting and citing sources, including documentation models, see Chapter 7.)

Note: One practice that will help you avoid plagiarism is to keep all of your research notes and rough drafts in separate files. Then, as you prepare your final draft, you will be able to check your notes if you are uncertain about whether a particular phrase is a direct quotation or a paraphrase, or where an idea or a quotation came from. (See 5d for more on careful note taking.) As noted in Chapter 5, a number of useful online citation tools can help you build your bibliography and create citations. These tools can also help you keep track of the sources you have quoted or consulted. Zotero (www .zotero.org), EndNote (www.endnote.com), and RefWorks (www.refworks.com) are all useful sites. You should, however, always check citations generated by a citation engine, as they are not always formatted correctly.

6b-2 Paraphrasing to avoid plagiarism

Most students know that copying a passage word for word from a source is plagiarism. However, many are unsure about how to paraphrase. Consider, for example, this passage from a recent book on the history of food and the unacceptable student paraphrase that follows.

ORIGINAL PASSAGE

The slave trade destroyed families, killed spiritual expression, and undermined the material world of transplanted Africans. This cultural holocaust was comprehensive, ruinous, and unrelenting. Remarkably, however, slaves refused to acquiesce to the brutality completely. They refused to sacrifice their basic sense of humanity. In fact, faced with such adversity, West Indian slaves discovered unique ways to forge a culture that blended their African heritage with New World conditions, however desperate those conditions may have been. Cast adrift in a sea of violence and greed, they sought, against all odds, to cling to at least a semblance of their inherited traditions. The most notable of these traditions was culinary.[1]

UNACCEPTABLE PARAPHRASE

Slavery ruined families, destroyed religious expression, and damaged the material world of the Africans who were brought to the West Indies. This cultural destruction was complete and unending.

1. James E. McWilliams, *A Revolution in Eating: How the Quest for Food Shaped America* (New York: Columbia University Press, 2005), 29–30.

Amazingly, however, slaves didn't give in. They refused to sacrifice
their basic sense of being human. In fact, faced with such hardships,
they found unique ways to make a new culture that brought together
their African heritage with conditions in the New World. In spite of
violence and greed, they tried to hold on to their inherited traditions.
The most notable of these traditions was food.

In this example, the writer's attempt at paraphrase results
in plagiarism, *despite the fact* that the second text is not
an exact copy of the original. First, the writer has not
acknowledged the source of his information; even though
there is no direct quotation, a citation is required. Second, this paragraph would be considered plagiarism *even
if* the writer acknowledged the source of the material by
including a citation. The writer has used a thesaurus to
find synonyms for several words—*destroyed* has become
ruined, comprehensive has been replaced by *complete*, and
hardships has been substituted for *adversity*. In addition,
several words or phrases in the original have been left
out in the second version, and the original word order
has occasionally been rearranged. Nevertheless, these
changes are merely editorial. The new paragraph is not
significantly different from the original in either form or
substance; it is simply too close to the original to be considered the work of the student.

To write a genuine paraphrase, you need to think about
what the source says and absorb it. Once you understand the content of the source, you can restate it in an
entirely original way that reflects your own wording and
style. Consider, for example, this paraphrase of the same
passage.

ACCEPTABLE PARAPHRASE

According to historian James McWilliams, the slave trade had a devastating effect on the family structure, religious practices, and way of
life of the Africans who were brought to the West Indies. Despite the
incredible hardships they endured, however, these men and women
managed to adapt elements of their traditional practices to the new,
and often terrible, circumstances of their lives as enslaved people. In
this process of building a new cultural identity, McWilliams argues,
food played a central role.[2]

    2. James E. McWilliams, *A Revolution in Eating: How the Quest
for Food Shaped America* (New York: Columbia University Press, 2005),
29–30.

This paraphrase is more successful; the writer has assimilated the content of the source and expressed it in his own words, relaying to the reader his understanding of what McWilliams said. You should also note that the writer has indicated the source of his information by using signal phrases such as "according to historian James McWilliams" and "McWilliams argues." Finally, even though the writer has not used any direct quotations and has mentioned his source by name in the text, he has also provided a footnote indicating the exact source of his information. Without this citation, this paraphrase would be considered plagiarism. (You can find detailed information about how to cite sources in Chapter 7.)

You will save time if you paraphrase as you take notes. However, if you attempt to paraphrase while looking at the original text, you are courting disaster. To write a genuine paraphrase, you should look away from the text and summarize in your own words what you have read. Then, go back and check the original source to make sure that you have not committed plagiarism by using language or

Tips for Writers
Avoiding Plagiarism

If . . .		Then . . .
The information is common knowledge	→	You do not need a citation
The *words* are your own **and** The *idea* is your own	→	You do not need a citation
The *words* are someone else's	→	Place them in quotation marks **and** Include a citation
The *words* are your own **but** The *idea* is someone else's	→	Acknowledge the author of the idea by referring to him/her in the text **and** Include a citation

Note: This chart is adapted from *Academic Honesty, Plagiarism, and the Honor System: A Handbook for Students* (Washington, DC: Trinity Washington University, 2005), 2, and is used by permission of Trinity Washington University.

sentence structure that closely matches the original. See the Tips for Writers box on page 109 for ways to avoid plagiarism. (For advice on taking notes in the form of summaries, see 3b-1. Another example of acceptable paraphrasing can be found on pp. 113–14.)

6b-3 Downloading internet sources carefully to avoid plagiarism

As with any other source, information derived from the internet must be properly paraphrased and cited. A particular danger arises, however, from the ease with which internet material can be downloaded into your working text. Whenever you download material from the internet, be sure to create a separate document file for that material. Otherwise, internet material may inadvertently become mixed up with your own writing. Moreover, keep in mind that websites are more volatile than print sources. Material on many websites is updated daily, and a site that you find early in your research may be revised or even completely gone by the time you write your final draft. Therefore, you should always record complete bibliographic information for each internet source as you use it, as well as the date on which you accessed the site.

6c   Plagiarism and the internet

While plagiarism is not a new problem, the opportunities for plagiarism have increased exponentially with the growing popularity of and dependence on the internet. Careless cut-and-paste practices, as noted above, pose a real hazard to unwary internet users. A more distressing and significant problem, however, is the virtual explosion of websites offering students the opportunity to buy term papers or even download them for free. Often presenting themselves as sources of "research assistance," these sites afford countless possibilities for plagiarism under the guise of providing "help" to students who are "in a hurry," "under pressure," or "working on a deadline." Many of these websites bury in the "FAQs" (Frequently Asked Questions) or "About Us" sections the caveat that students should use the website's papers only as "models" for their own papers. They are, of course, quite right to include this warning. However, before you decide to use the "research assistance" these websites claim to provide, consider the criteria for evaluating internet sources provided in Chapter 2 (see 2b-3).

If you are allowed and/or expected to incorporate web-based material into your research, you need to take special care to make certain that the sites you are using are reliable. In determining the usefulness of a website, you should always ask about the author's credentials; for many of these "paper mill" sites, the author of the paper is anonymous and may even be another student. Why, then, should you trust the information the paper provides? Similarly, the website's URL should cause you to hesitate; paper mills typically have a *.com* extension, rather than the more trustworthy *.edu* or *.gov* extension that you might expect from a true academic site. You should also consider whether you would really want to list the site in your bibliography; your professor probably will not be impressed with a bibliography entry for "schoolisrotten.com."

Finally, if you are ever tempted, you should also realize that if you found that website, no doubt your professor can find it too. It is not very hard—indeed, it is quite simple—for a professor to track down the source of a plagiarized paper. And remember: the consequences can be devastating.

Note: Ignorance about what constitutes plagiarism is not usually considered an acceptable excuse by college professors, school judicial associations, or university administrators. Read your school's policy on plagiarism and make sure you understand it. Finally, if you have any doubts or need clarification, ask your professors or consult a reference librarian.

7

Quoting and Documenting Sources

Any history paper you write reflects your careful reading and analysis of primary and secondary sources. This section offers general guidance on incorporating source material into your writing through quotation and paraphrase. It also explains the conventions historians use to cite and document sources.

7a Using quotations

Quotations are an important part of writing in history. Quotations from primary sources provide evidence and support for your thesis. Quotations from secondary sources tell your readers that you are well informed about the current state of research on the issue that you are examining. The guidelines that follow will help you decide when to quote and how to use quotations effectively.

7a-1 When to quote

Some students go to extremes, producing papers that are little more than a series of quotations loosely strung together. No matter how interesting and accurate the quotations, such a paper is no substitute for your own analysis and discussion of sources. In general, you should minimize your use of quotations, and you should choose the quotations you do use with great care. When deciding if you should use a quotation, consider the following points.

Do not quote if you can paraphrase. Summarizing or paraphrasing in your own words is usually preferable to direct quotation; it demonstrates that you have digested the information from the source and made it your own. In particular, you should not quote directly if the quotation would provide only factual information. Examine this passage from *Slave Counterpoint*, a study of eighteenth-century African American culture.

ORIGINAL PASSAGE

Working alongside black women in the fields were boys and girls. Although the age at which a child entered the labor force varied from plantation to plantation, most masters in both Chesapeake and Lowcountry regarded the years of nine or ten as marking this threshold. . . . Black children, unlike their enslaved mothers, do not seem to have been singled out for any more onerous duties than their white counterparts. Those white children who left home to become servants in husbandry in early modern England generally did so at age thirteen to fourteen. However, they had probably been working for neighboring farmers on a nonresident basis from as young as seven.[1]

This passage contains a number of interesting facts. However, while it is clear and well written, there is nothing particularly significant about the wording of the passage per se; there are no striking analogies or turns of phrase that are especially memorable. For this reason, a paraphrase is preferable to a direct quotation. The paraphrase that follows includes the important facts from the original but puts them in the writer's own words. As with all paraphrases, the model below includes a footnote to indicate the source of the information.

PARAPHRASE

Slave children began to work in the fields with their mothers at around the age of nine or ten. Their experiences as child laborers were similar to those of white children who worked in rural settings in England, where children as young as seven were sent to work on nearby farms, and moved into the homes of their employers in their early teens.[2]

---

2. Philip D. Morgan, *Slave Counterpoint: Black Culture in the Eighteenth-Century Chesapeake and Lowcountry* (Chapel Hill: University of North Carolina Press, 1998), 197.

For additional information on paraphrasing without plagiarizing, see 6b-2.

---

1. Philip D. Morgan, *Slave Counterpoint: Black Culture in the Eighteenth-Century Chesapeake and Lowcountry* (Chapel Hill: University of North Carolina Press, 1998), 197.

Do quote if the words of the original are especially memorable.
You might want to quote directly when your source says
something in a particularly striking way. Consider, for
example, the following passage from a student paper on
the cholera outbreak of 1854.

> Steven Johnson argues that the densely packed population of London
> provided ideal conditions for cholera bacteria to thrive. "London," he
> says, "offered *Vibrio cholerae* . . . precisely what it offered stock-bro-
> kers and coffee-house proprietors and sewer-hunters: a whole new way
> of making a living."[3]

> 3. Steven Johnson, *The Ghost Map: The Story of London's Most
> Terrifying Epidemic — and How It Changed Science, Cities, and the
> Modern World* (New York: Riverhead Books, 2006), 96.

Johnson's quotation is memorable because of his use of
analogy and anthropomorphism, which creates an image
that could not be duplicated in a summary or paraphrase.
The student, then, has chosen an effective quotation.

You might also wish to quote when the original words
are important to readers' understanding of the author's
intentions or feelings, as in the following example.

> Fire was a serious danger in sixteenth-century cities. Entire neigh-
> borhoods could be destroyed as a result of a single fire that grew out
> of control. In fact, victims of violent crime knew that they should
> call "Fire" rather than "Help" if they hoped someone would come to
> the rescue. As A. Roger Ekirch puts it, "If murder or robbery failed to
> animate their [neighbors'] sense of community, the threat of being
> burned alive almost always did."[4]

> 4. A. Roger Ekirch, *At Day's Close: Night in Times Past* (New York:
> W. W. Norton, 2005), 117.

In the quotation that ends this passage, the tone is as
important as the content. It would be impossible to
capture in a summary or paraphrase the irony of the
original.

7a-2 How to quote

When you quote, you must follow the conventions for
using quotation marks and integrating quotations in the
text of your paper. Keep in mind the following important
points.

Indicate where your quotation begins and ends. When quot-ing a source, you should quote the source's words exactly, and you should enclose the material from your source in quotation marks.

Frame your quotation. Quotations from sources cannot simply be dropped into your paper. Even if a quotation is properly cited (see 7b) and appropriate to a point you are making, you cannot assume that your readers will immediately grasp where the quotation comes from or why it is relevant. Therefore, you must contextualize the quotation by introducing the quotation and explaining its significance in your own words. This example is from a student paper on Judge Benjamin Lindsey, the founder of the first juvenile court in the United States.

INEFFECTIVE

Like most progressives, Lindsey was interested in social reform. "I found no 'problem of the children' that was not also the problem of their parents."[5]

---

5. Benjamin Barr Lindsey, *The Beast* (New York: Doubleday, 1910), 151.

In this example, the quotation is not clearly linked to the writer's statement that Lindsey was interested in social reform. Are readers meant to assume that Lindsey wanted to remove children from the homes of unfit parents? Pro-vide government support for indigent parents? Encourage state-funded family counseling?

In the revised version, the student clearly introduces the quotation and frames it in a way that makes its sig-nificance clear.

EFFECTIVE

Addressing the source of juvenile crime, Lindsey wrote: "I found no 'problem of the children' that was not also the problem of their par-ents."[6] Thus, for Lindsey, the reform of the juvenile justice system was intrinsically linked to the reform of adult criminal courts.

---

6. Benjamin Barr Lindsey, *The Beast* (New York: Doubleday, 1910), 151.

In this revision, the significance of the quotation as it pertains to the writer's argument is clear. The writer's analysis before and after the quotation puts Lindsey's words in context.

Integrate your quotations grammatically.   When you use a direct quotation, make sure that the resulting sentence is still grammatically correct. You may need to change an initial capital to lowercase, make a singular into a plural (or vice versa), or add a word or phrase to make the meaning of the original clear in the context of your sentence. If you need to change or add a letter or word, use brackets to indicate the change. For example, in the quotation from A. Roger Ekirch on page 114, the antecedent of the pronoun *their* was no longer clear when the quotation was taken out of its original context, so the writer has added the word *neighbors'* in brackets.

Note: You should not correct the grammar or spelling of the text you are quoting, particularly since not all "mistakes" are really errors. Older documents may use antiquated spellings (for example, "faerie" for "fairy"); spelling conventions also vary by country (for example, the American "color" is spelled "colour" in Great Britain and Canada). If, however, a source contains a genuine misspelling (and particularly if the reader might think that you are at fault for careless note taking), you can insert the Latin word *sic* in brackets to indicate that the mistake occurs in the original (see 5d).

Keep quotations brief.   To keep quoted material to a minimum, you should condense quoted passages by using ellipsis points (three periods, with spaces between), which indicate that you have left out some of the original material. The passage quoting Steven Johnson on page 114 includes an example of this method. If you are leaving out material at the end of a sentence you are quoting but what remains is a grammatically complete sentence, you do not need to use ellipsis points. If, however, you are omitting a sentence *within* a multi-sentence quotation, you should first type a period (with no space preceding it) at the end of the sentence and then three evenly spaced ellipsis points to indicate that material is missing before the next sentence. The passage quoting Chang Han on page 117 includes an example of this method.

Indent long quotations.   If your quotation is four or more typed lines, you should set it off by indenting it; this is called a block quotation. Block quotations are not enclosed in quotation marks. Typically, long quotations are preceded by an introductory sentence followed by a colon, as in this example:

The comments of Chang Han, an official of the Ming dynasty, reflect the attitude of many of his contemporaries toward outsiders:

> Foreigners are recalcitrant and their greed knows no bounds.
> . . . What is more, the greedy heart is unpredictable. If one day they break the treaties and invade our frontiers, who will be able to defend us against them?[7]

Despite this distrust, Jesuit missionaries were able to achieve positions of honor and trust in the imperial court, ultimately serving the emperor as scholars and advisers.

---

7. Chang Han, "Essay on Merchants," trans. Lily Hwa, in *Chinese Civilization and Society: A Sourcebook,* ed. Patricia Buckley Ebrey (New York: Free Press, 1981), 157.

You should use block quotations sparingly. Frequent use of long quotations suggests that you have not really understood the material well enough to paraphrase. Moreover, a long quotation can be distracting and cause readers to lose the thread of your argument. Use a lengthy quotation only if you have a compelling reason to do so.

Use quotation marks with other punctuation correctly. Commas and periods should always be enclosed within the quotation marks; colons and semicolons should appear outside the quotation marks; other end punctuation (question marks and exclamation points) should be enclosed within the quotation marks if they are part of the quotation and should appear outside if not.

Note: Footnote or endnote numbers should be placed outside quotation marks.

7b Documenting sources

For all the sources in your paper, including visual and other nonwritten materials, you must provide complete bibliographic information. This is important for two reasons. First, citing your sources gives them appropriate credit. Second, bibliographic information enables readers to look up your sources to evaluate your interpretation of them or to read more extensively from them.

7b-1   Footnotes and endnotes

Historians typically use footnotes or endnotes to document their sources. With this method, you place a raised number, called a *superscript*, at the end of the last word of a quotation, paraphrase, or summary. This number corresponds to a numbered note that provides bibliographic information about your source. Notes may be placed at the bottom of the page (footnotes) or at the end of the paper (endnotes). In either case, notes should be numbered consecutively from the beginning to the end of the paper. The following example shows a source cited in the body of a paper and documented in a footnote or endnote.

TEXT

Norton argues that "the witchcraft crisis of 1692 can be comprehended only in the context of nearly two decades of armed conflict between English settlers and the New England Indians."[8]

NOTE

8. Mary Beth Norton, *In the Devil's Snare: The Salem Witchcraft Crisis of 1692* (New York: Alfred A. Knopf, 2002), 12.

You should ask your instructor if he or she has a preference for footnotes or endnotes. If the choice is left up to you, weigh the advantages and disadvantages of each form. Footnotes allow your readers to refer easily and quickly to the sources cited on a given page, but they can be distracting. Further, historians often use explanatory or discursive notes, which contain more than simple bibliographic information. (For an example of a discursive endnote, see endnote 3 from the model student paper on p. 154.) If your paper has a large number of discursive footnotes, the pages might look overwhelmed with notes. If you use endnotes, you do not need to worry about their length. However, endnotes are less accessible, requiring readers to turn to the end of the paper to refer to each note. This is not, of course, a problem with papers submitted electronically, since the reader can access the note by clicking on the superscript.

7b-2   Bibliography

Papers with footnotes or endnotes also need to have a bibliography—a list of all the sources consulted or cited in the paper, arranged alphabetically by authors' last

names (or by title where there is no author). In a paper
with endnotes, the bibliography always follows the last
endnote page. (See p. 155 for a sample bibliography.)

Note: An alternative form of documentation commonly
used in professional journals in the social sciences is the
author-date system. The author's last name and the publication date of a cited source are included in parentheses in the text itself; complete bibliographic information
appears in a reference list at the end of the text. This form
of documentation is not often used in history because
the author-date system is generally not practical for documenting many of the primary sources historians use.
Occasionally, a history professor may suggest the use of
the author-date system for a book review or for a paper
citing only one or two sources, but you should not use it
unless you are specifically told to do so.

7b-3 Documenting nonwritten materials

Maps, graphs, photographs, cartoons, and other nonwritten materials can be useful in a history paper. It is not
enough, however, to add these materials to your paper
without discussion or explanation. When they appear
in the body of a paper, visual materials, like quotations,
should be incorporated into the text. Each image should
include a caption that identifies it, and the text accompanying any visual material should explain its significance and its relationship to the topic of discussion. If
you group visual materials in an appendix to your paper,
you will also need to supply captions that identify the
materials and their sources. Of course, using maps, photographs, and other nonwritten materials without full
citations constitutes plagiarism. Like any other source,
nonwritten materials must be cited in the bibliography.
(See documentation model 21 on p. 131.)

7c Documentation models

The models in this section follow the notes and bibliography system set forth by *The Chicago Manual of Style*, 17th
ed. (Chicago: University of Chicago Press, 2017). The *Chicago* system is the format usually preferred by historians
and the one your history instructor will most likely ask
you to follow. If you are uncertain, check your syllabus or
ask your instructor for his or her preference.

Directory to Documentation Models

7c-1 Formatting guidelines for footnotes and endnotes

As noted in 7b, historians provide notes, either at the bottom of each page (footnotes) or at the end of a text (endnotes), to acknowledge their sources and enable their readers to find the same sources for themselves. The following example illustrates the elements that should be included in a typical note when a source is referenced for the first time. Models for citing specific sources follow in 7c-3.

1. First reference to a source
All notes begin with a paragraph indent and are numbered consecutively throughout the paper. Individual notes should be single-spaced, with a double space between notes. When a source is noted for the first time, you should include complete bibliographic information.

1. Anne Salmond, *Aphrodite's Island: The European Discovery of Tahiti* (Berkeley: University of California Press, 2009), 316.

2. Shortened forms in subsequent notes
As illustrated above, the first time you cite a source, you *must* provide complete bibliographic information. In subsequent notes, however, use a shortened form: cite the author's last name, followed by a comma; the key words from the main title; and the page or pages cited.

2. Salmond, *Aphrodite's Island*, 73.

7c-2 Formatting guidelines for bibliographies

Your bibliography is a list of the books, articles, and other sources you used in preparing your paper. It must include all the works you cited in your notes; it may also include other works that you consulted but did not cite. However, avoid the temptation to pad your bibliography; list only materials you did in fact use.

Note: If your bibliography is long, you may wish to divide it into sections, such as "Primary Sources" and "Books and Articles." If you have used manuscripts or other unpublished sources, you might list these separately as well.

3. Typical bibliography entry

The following example illustrates the elements that should be included in a typical bibliography entry. Models for citing a variety of specific sources can be found in 7c-3.

Salmond, Anne. *Aphrodite's Island: The European Discovery of Tahiti.*
    Berkeley: University of California Press, 2009.

Bibliography entries are listed alphabetically by authors' last names; the first line of the entry begins at the far left, and subsequent lines are indented. Each author is listed last name first, followed by a comma and then the first name and initial(s) (if any). Periods separate the author's name, title of the work, and publication information. Individual entries should be single-spaced, with a double space between entries.

4. Multiple works by the same author

If your bibliography includes more than one work by the same author, use a 3-em dash in place of the author's name in subsequent bibliography entries. (If you are using a Windows OS, create a 3-em dash by pressing Alt + 0151 on the math keypad. If you are using a Mac OS, press Shift + Alt + the hyphen key). List books by the same author alphabetically by title.

Salmond, Anne. *Aphrodite's Island: The European Discovery of Tahiti.*
    Berkeley: University of California Press, 2009.

—. *The Trial of the Cannibal Dog: The Remarkable Story of Captain Cook's
    Encounters in the South Seas.* New Haven, CT: Yale University Press,
    2003.

7c-3   Models for notes and bibliography entries

The following documentation models of notes and bibliography entries illustrate the types of sources commonly used in history. The Directory to Documentation Models on page 120 lists the various types of sources and the page numbers where the models can be found. For each source, the model note appears first, followed by a bibliography entry for the same source. Pay careful attention to the differences in formatting between these two forms of citation.

- An "N" in the margin signifies that the model is formatted as a footnote or an endnote.
- A "B" in the margin indicates a bibliography format.

For additional help with formatting notes and bibliography entries, see 7c-1 and 7c-2.

A Note on Citing Electronic Sources: Online sources are identified by their URL, or Uniform Resource Locator. However, since URLs are not always stable, books and articles are sometimes assigned a permanent DOI, or Digital Object Identifier (you will most often find one for articles accessed through online databases). If a DOI is available, you should cite it instead of the URL. If a DOI or URL is long and you need to break it at the end of a line, make the break *after* a colon or double slash but *before* any other punctuation marks.

The Chicago Manual of Style does not recommend including access dates (the date on which you consulted a source) unless the publication or modification date cannot be determined. If your professor asks you to include the access date, it should come before the URL or DOI.

Books (print and online)

5. Basic form for a book

Include the author's name, the complete title (including subtitle) in italics, the place of publication, the publisher's name, and the publication date. (The Citation Guide on p. 126 illustrates how to find these elements in a book and list them in the correct order.) Give page numbers for footnotes and endnotes, but not for bibliography entries.

N   5. Christopher J. Greig, *Ontario Boys: Masculinity and the Ideas of Boyhood in Postwar Ontario, 1945–1960* (Waterloo, Ontario: Wilfrid Laurier University Press, 2014), 97–98.

B   Greig, Christopher J. *Ontario Boys: Masculinity and the Ideas of Boyhood in Postwar Ontario, 1945–1960*. Waterloo, Ontario: Wilfrid Laurier University Press, 2014.

6. E-book (Electronic book)

For e-books, include all of the standard publication information available as you would for a print book. Because electronic editions may vary from their print counterparts, you should indicate the format for books downloaded from a library or an online bookseller. Since the pagination of e-books may vary, include the chapter number or another locator instead of page numbers.

N   6. Michael T. Rock, *Dictators, Democrats, and Development in Southeast Asia: Implications for the Rest* (Oxford: Oxford University Press, 2016), chap. 2, Kindle edition.

B   Rock, Michael T. Dictators, *Democrats, and Development in Southeast Asia: Implications for the Rest*. Oxford: Oxford University Press, 2016. Kindle edition.

7. Book accessed online

If you are citing a free online book, you should also cite the online publisher; the date of publication online, if known; and the URL (or DOI, if available).

N   7. Alfred Russel Wallace, *Contributions to the Theory of Natural Selection: A Series of Essays* (New York: Macmillan, 1871; Project Gutenberg, 2007), http://www.gutenberg.org/etext/22428.

B   Wallace, Alfred Russel. *Contributions to the Theory of Natural Selection: A Series of Essays*. New York: Macmillan, 1871; Project Gutenberg, 2007. http://www.gutenberg.org/etext/22428.

If you have accessed an online book through an authored website, your note should also include the author, name, and date of the website, if known.

N   7. Cotton Mather, *Memorable Providences, Relating to Witchcrafts and Possessions* (1689), at Douglas O. Linder, *Famous Trials*, http://www.law.umkc.edu/faculty/projects/ftrials/salem/ASA_MATH.HTM.

B   Mather, Cotton. *Memorable Providences, Relating to Witchcrafts and Possessions*. 1689. At Douglas O. Linder. *Famous Trials*. http://www.law.umkc.edu/faculty/projects/ftrials/salem/ASA _MATH.HTM.

8. Two or more authors

List the authors in your note in the order in which their names appear on the title page. In a bibliography entry, list the first author's name in reverse order (last name first), but give the names of the other authors in the normal order.

N   8. Matthew Carotenuto and Katherine Luongo, *Obama and Kenya: Contested Histories and the Politics of Belonging* (Athens, Ohio: Ohio University Press, 2016), 169.

B   Carotenuto, Matthew, and Matthew M. Heaton. *Obama and Kenya: Contested Histories and the Politics of Belonging*. Athens, Ohio: Ohio University Press, 2016.

Note: For a book with more than three authors, you may use the Latin term *et al.* ("and others") after the first author instead of listing all the authors in a footnote or endnote (for example, Jane Doe et al.). Bibliography entries, however, must include all of the authors' names.

9. Author's name in the title
When an author's name appears in the title of a book, as in a collection of letters or papers, your footnote or endnote should begin with the title of the book.

N   9. *The Letters of Sylvia Beach,* ed. Keri Walsh (New York: Columbia University Press, 2010), 115–19.

Begin the bibliography entry with the author's name, even if it appears in the title.

B   Beach, Sylvia. *The Letters of Sylvia Beach*. Edited by Keri Walsh. New York: Columbia University Press, 2010.

10. Anonymous work
For works with no known author, editor, or compiler, begin with the title.

N   10. *A Workingman's Ideas of Conscription (1917)* (Whitefish, MT: Kessinger, 2010), 83.

In the bibliography, list the work by its title. If the title begins with an article (*a*, *an*, or *the*), alphabetize the book according to the first letter of the next word.

B   *A Workingman's Ideas of Conscription (1917)*. Whitefish, MT: Kessinger, 2010.

Citation Guide
Books

A typical citation for a book includes the information below, available from the title page and copyright page. In addition, page number(s) are included for notes but not for bibliography entries. See the next page for the corresponding note and bibliography entries, along with formatting tips.

1 Author

2 Title and subtitle

5 Date of publication

Copyright © 1999

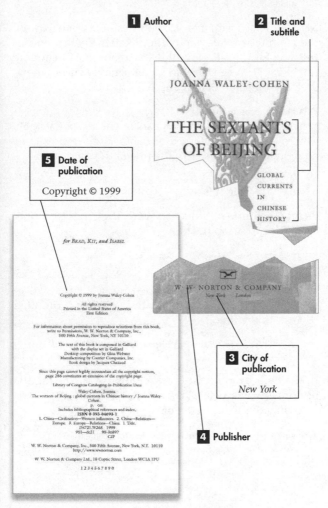

JOANNA WALEY-COHEN

THE SEXTANTS OF BEIJING

GLOBAL CURRENTS IN CHINESE HISTORY

for BRAD, KIT, and ISABEL

Copyright © 1999 by Joanna Waley-Cohen

All rights reserved
Printed in the United States of America
First Edition

For information about permission to reproduce selections from this book,
write to Permissions, W. W. Norton & Company, Inc.,
500 Fifth Avenue, New York, NY 10110.

The text of this book is composed in Galliard
with the display set in Galliard
Desktop composition by Gina Webster
Manufacturing by Courier Companies, Inc.
Book design by Jacques Chazaud

Since this page cannot legibly accommodate all the copyright notices,
page 286 constitutes an extension of the copyright page.

Library of Congress Cataloging-in-Publication Data
Waley-Cohen, Joanna.
The sextants of Beijing : global currents in Chinese history / Joanna Waley-Cohen.
p. cm.
Includes bibliographical references and index.
ISBN 0-393-04693-1
1. China—Civilization—Western influences. 2. China—Relations—Europe. 3. Europe—Relations—China. I. Title.
DS721.W268 1999
951—dc21   98-36897
CIP

W. W. Norton & Company, Inc., 500 Fifth Avenue, New York, N.Y. 10110
http://www.wwnorton.com

W. W. Norton & Company Ltd., 10 Coptic Street, London WC1A 1PU

1 2 3 4 5 6 7 8 9 0

W. W. NORTON & COMPANY
New York   London

3 City of publication

New York

4 Publisher

126

Note

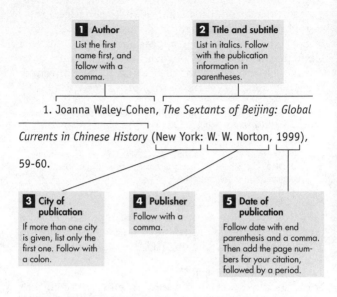

1 **Author**
List the first name first, and follow with a comma.

2 **Title and subtitle**
List in italics. Follow with the publication information in parentheses.

1. Joanna Waley-Cohen, *The Sextants of Beijing: Global Currents in Chinese History* (New York: W. W. Norton, 1999), 59-60.

3 **City of publication**
If more than one city is given, list only the first one. Follow with a colon.

4 **Publisher**
Follow with a comma.

5 **Date of publication**
Follow date with end parenthesis and a comma. Then add the page numbers for your citation, followed by a period.

Bibliography

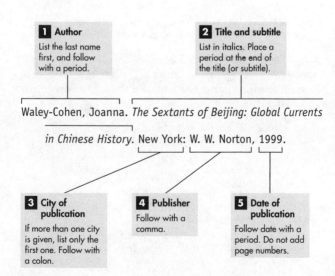

1 **Author**
List the last name first, and follow with a period.

2 **Title and subtitle**
List in italics. Place a period at the end of the title (or subtitle).

Waley-Cohen, Joanna. *The Sextants of Beijing: Global Currents in Chinese History.* New York: W. W. Norton, 1999.

3 **City of publication**
If more than one city is given, list only the first one. Follow with a colon.

4 **Publisher**
Follow with a comma.

5 **Date of publication**
Follow date with a period. Do not add page numbers.

11. Edited book without an author

Sometimes (as, for example, with a collection or anthology) a book may not list an author on its title page. In this case, cite the book by its editor (*ed.*) or editors (*eds.*), listed in the order in which they appear on the title page. In a bibliography entry for a book with multiple editors, as in this model, only the name of the first editor is inverted; the others are given in the normal order.

N 11. Benjamin E. Zeller, Marie W. Dallam, Reid L. Neilson, and Nora L. Rubel, eds., *Religion, Food, and Eating in North America* (New York: Columbia University Press, 2014), 312.

B Zeller, Benjamin E., Marie W. Dallam, Reid L. Neilson, and Nora L. Rubel, eds. *Religion, Food, and Eating in North America*. New York: Columbia University Press, 2014.

Note: A book with multiple editors should be treated the same way as a book with multiple authors (see model 8 on p. 124); list the editors (abbreviated *eds.*) in the order in which they appear on the title page.

12. Edited work with an author

For a book with an author and an editor, the editor's name follows the title.

N 12. Laura Ingalls Wilder, *The Selected Letters of Laura Ingalls Wilder*, ed. William Anderson (New York: HarperCollins Publishers, 2016), 321–22.

B Wilder, Laura Ingalls. *The Selected Letters of Laura Ingalls Wilder*. Edited by William Anderson. New York: HarperCollins Publishers, 2016.

13. Translated work

A translator's name, like an editor's, is placed after the title when an author's name is given. If a source has an editor and a translator, then list both.

N 13. Alex Carmel, *Ottoman Haifa: A History of Four Centuries under Turkish Rule*, trans. Elias Friedman (London: I. B. Tauris, 2011), 196.

B Carmel, Alex. *Ottoman Haifa: A History of Four Centuries under Turkish Rule*. Translated by Elias Friedman. London: I. B. Tauris, 2011.

N 13. Van Ngo, In the Crossfire: *Adventures of a Vietnamese Revolutionary*, ed. Ken Knabb and Hélène Fleury, trans. Hélène Fleury (Oakland, CA: AK Press, 2010), 27.

B Ngo, Van. In the Crossfire: *Adventures of a Vietnamese Revolutionary*. Edited by Ken Knabb and Hélène Fleury. Translated by Hélène Fleury. Oakland, CA: AK Press, 2010.

14. Multivolume work

If you are citing an individual volume of a multivolume work that does not have its own title, the note should include the volume number cited and the page numbers after the publication information. If your paper references two or more volumes, the bibliography entry should list the number of volumes in the work; if you reference only one of the volumes, the bibliography should list only the volume used.

N   14. Sita Anantha Raman, *Women in India: A Social and Cultural History* (Santa Barbara, CA: Praeger/ABC-CLIO, 2009), 1:150–51.

B   Raman, Sita Anantha. *Women in India: A Social and Cultural History.* 2 vols. Santa Barbara, CA: Praeger/ABC-CLIO, 2009.

If a single volume in a multivolume work has a separate title, include the volume number and title directly after the general title.

N   14. Marilyn French, *From Eve to Dawn: A History of Women*, vol. 1, *Origins* (New York: Feminist Press at the City University of New York, 2008), 76.

B   French, Marilyn. *From Eve to Dawn: A History of Women*. Vol. 1, *Origins*. New York: Feminist Press at the City University of New York, 2008.

15. Edition other than the first

If the text you are using is not the first edition, provide the edition number in your note and bibliography.

N   15. Tamara Sonn, *Islam: A Brief History*, 2nd ed. (Malden, MA: Wiley-Blackwell, 2010), 163.

B   Sonn, Tamara. *Islam: A Brief History*. 2nd ed. Malden, MA: Wiley-Blackwell, 2010.

16. Work in a series

Some books are part of a series: publications on the same general subject that are supervised by a general editor or group of editors. For such books, include the series title but not the name of the series editor(s).

N   16. Garth Stevenson, *Building Nations from Diversity: Canadian and American Experience Compared*, McGill-Queen's Studies in Ethnic History (Montreal: McGill-Queen's University Press, 2014), 75–76.

B   Stevenson, Garth. *Building Nations from Diversity: Canadian and American Experience Compared*. McGill-Queen's Studies in Ethnic History. Montreal: McGill-Queen's University Press, 2014.

Sections or documents within books

17. Foreword, preface, introduction, or afterword

If the author of the foreword, preface, introduction, or afterword is also the author of the book, include the title of the section you are citing (in lowercase) after the author's name and before the title. If you are citing an introduction or other material written by someone other than the author of the book, the writer you are citing is listed first. Include the part's full page number range in the bibliography entry, but only the page cited in the note entry.

N   17. Alister E. McGrath, introduction to *Darwinism and the Divine: Evolutionary Thought and Natural Theology* (Malden, MA: Wiley-Blackwell, 2011), 6.

B   McGrath, Alister E. *Darwinism and the Divine: Evolutionary Thought and Natural Theology*, 1–7. Malden, MA: Wiley-Blackwell, 2011.

N   17. Saurabh Kumar, foreword to *Ireland and India: Colonies, Culture, and Empire*, ed. Tadhg Foley and Maureen O'Connor (Portland, OR: Irish Academic Press, 2006), ix.

B   Kumar, Saurabh. Foreword to *Ireland and India: Colonies, Culture, and Empire*, ix–x. Edited by Tadhg Foley and Maureen O'Connor. Portland, OR: Irish Academic Press, 2006.

18. Article or chapter in an edited work

Cite the author and title of the chapter or article first, followed by the title, editor, and publication information for the book in which it appears. Include the specific page number you are citing in the note and the complete range of page numbers for the article in the bibliography.

N   18. Raul Molina Mejia, "Bringing Justice to Guatemala: The Need to Confront Genocide and Other Crimes against Humanity," in *State Violence and Genocide in Latin America: The Cold War Years*, ed. Marcia Esparza, Henry R. Huttenbach, and Daniel Feierstein (London: Routledge, 2010), 223–24.

B   Mejia, Raul Molina. "Bringing Justice to Guatemala: The Need to Confront Genocide and Other Crimes against Humanity." In *State Violence and Genocide in Latin America: The Cold War Years*, edited by Marcia Esparza, Henry R. Huttenbach, and Daniel Feierstein, 209–34. London: Routledge, 2010.

19. Letter in a published collection

List the sender, recipient, and date of the communication, and then cite the collection as you would a book. Include the page number(s) in the note but not in the bibliography entry. The Citation Guide on page 132 illustrates how to find all of these elements from a primary text in a collection and put them in the correct order.

N   19. Private Arthur E. Stark to Carole Joyce Stark Blocker, 2 January 1944, in *World War II Letters: A Glimpse into the Heart of the Second World War through the Words of Those Who Were Fighting It,* ed. Bill Adler (New York: St. Martin's Press, 2002), 142.

If you cite only one letter from a collection, you may list it as an individual letter in your bibliography, beginning with the author's last name.

B   Stark, Arthur E. Private Arthur E. Stark to Carole Joyce Stark Blocker, 2 January 1944. In *World War II Letters: A Glimpse into the Heart of the Second World War through the Words of Those Who Were Fighting It,* edited by Bill Adler. New York: St. Martin's Press, 2002.

If you cite several letters from the same collection, however, list only the collection in your bibliography.

B   Adler, Bill, ed. *World War II Letters: A Glimpse into the Heart of the Second World War through the Words of Those Who Were Fighting It.* New York: St. Martin's Press, 2002.

20. Other primary source in a published collection

Other than letters, *The Chicago Manual of Style*, 17th ed., does not provide specific guidance on how to cite primary sources contained in published collections, but the guidelines in model 18 will work in most situations. The titles of reprinted book-length works such as pamphlets or plays should be in italics, not quotation marks. In some cases, it may also be helpful to provide the original date of the source (if known). The following example is for a seventeenth-century pamphlet reprinted in a book.

N   20. William Walwyn, *Toleration Justified and Persecution Condemned* (1646), in *The English Levellers,* ed. Andrew Sharp (Cambridge: Cambridge University Press, 1998), 26–27.

B   Walwyn, William. *Toleration Justified and Persecution Condemned.* 1646. In *The English Levellers,* edited by Andrew Sharp, 9–30. Cambridge: Cambridge University Press, 1998.

21. Illustration, table, or map

Information about visual sources is usually provided in the text or in a caption. If you need to supply a footnote, include the name of the person who made the item and its title, if available, followed by complete bibliographic information for the book or website in which it appears. In the note, give both the page number on which the item appears and any accompanying map, figure, table, or other number.

N   21. Meighan Cavanaugh, *The Venetian World* (map), in *Thomas F. Madden, Venice: A New History,* (New York: Viking, 2012), xii–xiii.

B   Cavanaugh, Meighan. *The Venetian World* (map). In *Thomas F. Madden. Venice: A New History.* New York: Viking, 2012, xii–xiii.

Citation Guide
Letters in published collections

A typical citation for a letter in a published collection includes the information below. In addition, page number(s) are included for notes but not for bibliography entries. See the next page for the corresponding note and bibliography entries, along with formatting tips.

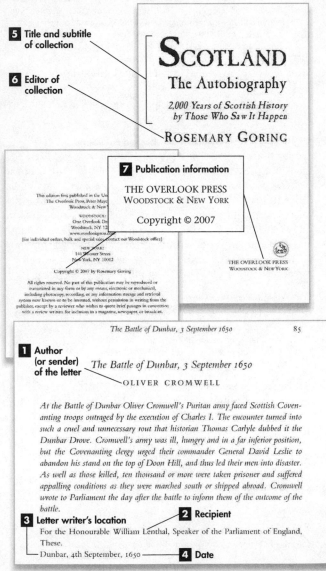

5 Title and subtitle of collection

6 Editor of collection

SCOTLAND
The Autobiography

2,000 Years of Scottish History
by Those Who Saw It Happen

ROSEMARY GORING

7 Publication information

THE OVERLOOK PRESS
WOODSTOCK & NEW YORK

Copyright © 2007

This edition first published in the Un...
The Overlook Press, Peter Maye...
Woodstock & New...

WOODSTOCK:
One Overlook Dr...
Woodstock, NY 12...
www.overlookpress.c...
[for individual orders, bulk and special sales, contact our Woodstock office]

NEW YORK:
141 Wooster Street
New York, NY 10012

Copyright © 2007 by Rosemary Goring

All rights reserved. No part of this publication may be reproduced or transmitted in any form or by any means, electronic or mechanical, including photocopy, recording, or any information storage and retrieval system now known or to be invented, without permission in writing from the publisher, except by a reviewer who wishes to quote brief passages in connection with a review written for inclusion in a magazine, newspaper, or broadcast.

THE OVERLOOK PRESS
WOODSTOCK & NEW YORK

The Battle of Dunbar, 3 September 1650   85

1 Author (or sender) of the letter

The Battle of Dunbar, 3 September 1650
OLIVER CROMWELL

At the Battle of Dunbar Oliver Cromwell's Puritan army faced Scottish Covenanting troops outraged by the execution of Charles I. The encounter turned into such a cruel and unnecessary rout that historian Thomas Carlyle dubbed it the Dunbar Drove. Cromwell's army was ill, hungry and in a far inferior position, but the Covenanting clergy urged their commander General David Leslie to abandon his stand on the top of Doon Hill, and thus led their men into disaster. As well as those killed, ten thousand or more were taken prisoner and suffered appalling conditions as they were marched south or shipped abroad. Cromwell wrote to Parliament the day after the battle to inform them of the outcome of the battle.

3 Letter writer's location   **2** Recipient

For the Honourable William Lenthal, Speaker of the Parliament of England, These.

Dunbar, 4th September, 1650 ———— **4** Date

132

Note

1 **Author (or sender) of the letter**
List the first name first, and follow with *to*.

2 **Recipient**
Follow with a comma.

3 **Letter writer's location**
Follow with a comma.

4 **Date**
Follow with a comma.

1. Oliver Cromwell to William Lenthal, Dunbar, 4 September 1650, in *Scotland, the Autobiography: 2,000 Years of Scottish History by Those Who Saw It Happen*, ed. Rosemary Goring (Woodstock, NY: Overlook Press, 2007), 85–88.

5 **Title and subtitle of collection**
List in italics, and precede with the word *in*. Follow title with a comma.

6 **Editor of collection**
Type *ed.* before the name of the editor.

7 **Publication information**
Enclose in parentheses. List the city (and state abbreviation, if necessary). Follow with a colon, the publisher, a comma, and the publication year. After the end parenthesis, add a comma, the page range for the entire letter, and a period.

Bibliography

1 **Author (or sender) of the letter**
List the last name first, and follow with a period. Then list the author's name again, first name first, and follow with the word *to*.

2 **Recipient**
Follow with a comma.

3 **Letter writer's location**
Follow with a comma.

4 **Date** Follow with a period.

Cromwell, Oliver. Oliver Cromwell to William Lenthal, Dunbar, 4 September 1650. In *Scotland, the Autobiography: 2,000 Years of Scottish History by Those Who Saw It Happen*, edited by Rosemary Goring. Woodstock, NY: Overlook Press, 2007.

5 **Title and subtitle of collection**
List in italics, and precede with the word *In*. Follow title with a comma.

6 **Editor of collection**
Type *edited by* before the name of the editor. Follow with a period.

7 **Publication information**
List the city (and the state abbreviation, if necessary). Follow with a colon, the publisher, a comma, and the publication date. Then add a period.

If the item does not have its own title or author, list your note and bibliography entry according to the author or editor of the book in which it appears.

22. A source quoted in another source

If material you wish to use from a source has been taken from another source, it is always preferable to find and consult the original source. If this is not possible, you must acknowledge *both* the original source of the material *and* your own source for the information.

N   22. E. W. Creak, "On the Mariner's Compass in Modern Vessels of War," *Journal of the Royal United Services Institute* 33 (1889–90): 966, quoted in Alan Gurney, *Compass: A Story of Exploration and Innovation* (New York: W. W. Norton, 2004), 275–76.

B   Creak, E. W. "On the Mariner's Compass in Modern Vessels of War." *Journal of the Royal United Services Institute* 33 (1889–90): 949–75. Quoted in Alan Gurney. *Compass: A Story of Exploration and Innovation*. New York: W. W. Norton, 2004.

Reference works

23. Dictionary or encyclopedia

In a note for a standard reference work that is arranged alphabetically, such as a dictionary or an encyclopedia, omit the publication information as well as the volume and page references. You must, however, note the edition if it is not the first. After the name and edition of the work, use the abbreviation *s.v.* (for *sub verbo*, "under the word") followed by the title of the entry in quotation marks.

N   23. *Encyclopedia Britannica*, 15th ed. rev. (1985), s.v. "steam power."

N   23. *Merriam-Webster's Collegiate Dictionary*, 11th ed. (2003), s.v. "civilization."

Well-known reference works are usually not included in bibliographies. For on-line reference works, which may be frequently updated, include the revision date, if known, or the access date, and the URL.

Specialized encyclopedias or dictionaries may contain lengthy entries written by identified authors; in this case, you should cite the entry as you would an article or a chapter in an edited book (see 18 on p. 130). Such articles should be listed in your bibliography.

N   23. William McKinley Runyan, "Henry Alexander Murray," in *New Dictionary of Scientific Biography*, ed. Noretta Koertge (New York: Charles Scribner's Sons, 2007).

B   Runyan, William McKinley. "Henry Alexander Murray." In *New Dictionary of Scientific Biography*, edited by Noretta Koertge. New York: Charles Scribner's Sons, 2007.

24. Sacred text

When referring to a passage from the Bible, cite the book (abbreviated), chapter, and verse(s), either in the text or in a note. Do not provide a page number. Identify the version in parentheses.

N   24. Matt. 20:4–9 (Revised Standard Version).

When referring to the Qur'an or other sacred work, use similar punctuation to refer to the parts of the text.

N   24. Qur'an 29:46.

Sacred texts are usually not included in bibliographies.

Periodicals (print and online)

25. Basic form for a journal article (print)

Include the author's name, the title of the article in quotation marks, the name of the journal in italics, the volume number, and the date in parentheses. (If an article has two or more authors, follow the style shown in model 8 for books with two or more authors on p. 124.) In the note, include the page number(s) for the specific material you are citing; in the bibliography, include all the page numbers for the article. The Citation Guide on page 136 illustrates how to find all of these elements from a journal article and put them in the correct order.

N   25. Jonathan Saha, "Murder at London Zoo: Late Colonial Sympathy in Interwar Britain," *The American Historical Review* 121 (December 2016): 1470–71.

B   Saha, Jonathan. "Murder at London Zoo: Late Colonial Sympathy in Interwar Britain." *The American Historical Review* 121 (December 2016): 1468–1491.

Some journals provide both volume and issue numbers. In the following model, the volume number is 49, the issue number is 1, the year of publication is 2014, and the page reference is 50–51.

N   25. Yves Frenette, "Conscripting Canada's Past: The Harper Government and the Politics of Memory," *Canadian Journal of History* 49, no. 1 (2014): 50–51.

B   Frenette, Yves. "Conscripting Canada's Past: The Harper Government and the Politics of Memory." *Canadian Journal of History* 49, no. 1 (2014): 49–65.

Note: You do not need to include the month or quarter of publication if you include the issue number, although it is not incorrect to do so.

Citation Guide
Articles in print journals

A typical citation for an article accessed in a print journal includes the information below. See the next page for the corresponding note and bibliography entries, along with formatting tips.

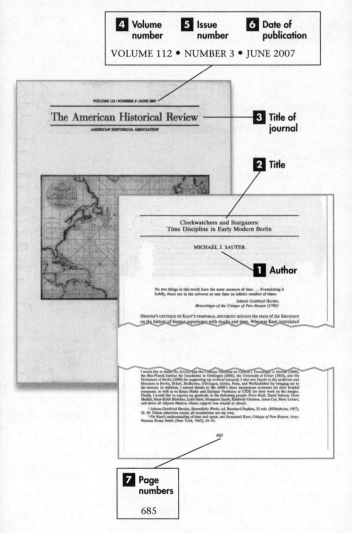

4 Volume number **5** Issue number **6** Date of publication

VOLUME 112 • NUMBER 3 • JUNE 2007

The American Historical Review
AMERICAN HISTORICAL ASSOCIATION

3 Title of journal

2 Title

Clockwatchers and Stargazers:
Time Discipline in Early Modern Berlin

MICHAEL J. SAUTER

1 Author

No two things in this world have the same measure of time . . . Formulating it boldly, there are in the universe at one time an infinite number of times.

Johann Gottfried Herder,
Metacritique of the Critique of Pure Reason (1799)¹

HERDER'S CRITIQUE OF KANT'S TEMPORAL ÆSTHETIC mirrors the state of the literature on the history of human experience with clocks and time. Whereas Kant postulated

I would like to thank the DAAD and the Consejo Nacional de Ciencia y Tecnología in Mexico (2006), the Max-Planck-Institut für Geschichte in Göttingen (2006), the University of Erfurt (2003), and the Parliament of Berlin (2000) for supporting my archival research. I also owe thanks to the archivists and librarians in Berlin, Erfurt, Heilbronn, Göttingen, Gotha, Paris, and Wolfenbüttel for bringing me to the sources. In addition, I extend thanks to the *AHR*'s three anonymous reviewers for their helpful comments, as well as to Katya Hinder and Enrique Verdusco at CIDE for their work on the images. Finally, I would like to express my gratitude to the following people: Peter Reill, David Sabean, Hans Medick, Hans-Erich Bödeker, Lynn Hunt, Margaret Jacob, Kimberly Garmoe, Jason Coy, Marc Lerner, and above all Allyson Brenton, whose support was crucial as always.

¹ Johann Gottfried Herder, *Sämmtliche Werke*, ed. Bernhard Suphan, 33 vols. (Hildesheim, 1967), 21: 59. Unless otherwise noted, all translations are my own.
² On Kant's understanding of time and space, see Immanuel Kant, *Critique of Pure Reason*, trans. Norman Kemp Smith (New York, 1965), 65–91.

685

7 Page numbers

685

136

Note

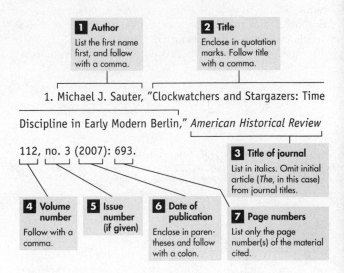

1. Michael J. Sauter, "Clockwatchers and Stargazers: Time Discipline in Early Modern Berlin," *American Historical Review* 112, no. 3 (2007): 693.

1 Author
List the first name first, and follow with a comma.

2 Title
Enclose in quotation marks. Follow title with a comma.

3 Title of journal
List in italics. Omit initial article (*The*, in this case) from journal titles.

4 Volume number
Follow with a comma.

5 Issue number (if given)

6 Date of publication
Enclose in parentheses and follow with a colon.

7 Page numbers
List only the page number(s) of the material cited.

Bibliography

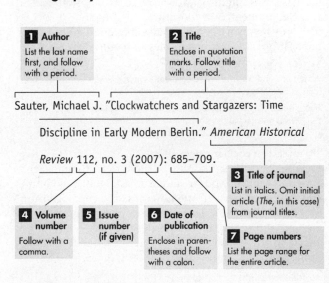

Sauter, Michael J. "Clockwatchers and Stargazers: Time Discipline in Early Modern Berlin." *American Historical Review* 112, no. 3 (2007): 685–709.

1 Author
List the last name first, and follow with a period.

2 Title
Enclose in quotation marks. Follow title with a period.

3 Title of journal
List in italics. Omit initial article (*The*, in this case) from journal titles.

4 Volume number
Follow with a comma.

5 Issue number (if given)

6 Date of publication
Enclose in parentheses and follow with a colon.

7 Page numbers
List the page range for the entire article.

26. Article in an online journal

Include the standard information for print articles: author's name; article title; journal title; volume number; publication date; page number(s), if available; and the DOI, if the article has one. If there is no DOI, include the URL. *Chicago* does not require the access date, but if your professor requests it, include it before the DOI or URL.

N   26. Thomas Lane, "Ethnic Diversity and Civil Nationalism: Estonia and Latvia in Comparative Perspective," *Central and Eastern European Review* 7 (2013): 14–15, http://spaces.brad.ac.uk :8080/download/ attachments/5079167/Lane.pdf?version1&modification Date=1372189546000.

B   Lane, Thomas. "Ethnic Diversity and Civil Nationalism: Estonia and Latvia in Comparative Perspective." *Central and Eastern European Review* 7 (2013): 1–20. http://spaces.brad.ac.uk:8080/download/ attachments/5079167/Lane.pdf?version=1 &modificationDate=1372189546000.

27. Article accessed from a database

Include the standard information for a print article (see model 25) in addition to the DOI, if the database provides one. If not, include the URL only if the database includes a stable form; otherwise, list the name of the database (for example, LexisNexis Academic) and any other identifying number assigned by the database. (Depending on the database, this might be called an "accession number," an "article number," or a "document id.") Include an access date only if you are citing a source that does not provide a publication date or if your professor requires it.

N   27. Andrew Jenks, "Model City USA: The Environmental Cost of Victory in World War II and the Cold War," *Environmental History* 12, no. 3 (2007): 563, http://www.jstor.org/stable/25473132.

B   Jenks, Andrew. "Model City USA: The Environmental Cost of Victory in World War II and the Cold War." *Environmental History* 12, no. 3 (2007): 552–77. http://www.jstor.org/stable /25473132.

28. Article in a popular magazine

Include the author, the title of the article, the magazine title, and the date (not in parentheses). Omit the volume and issue numbers. In the note, include the page number(s) of the specific material you are citing. You may, but are not required to, include the entire page range of the article in the bibliography; if you do, precede the page numbers with a comma, not a colon.

N   28. Ta-Nehisi Coates, "My President Was Black," *The Atlantic*, January/February 2017, 53.

B   Coates, Ta-Nehisi. "My President Was Black," *The Atlantic*, January/ February 2017, 46–66.

29. Newspaper article (print)

Cite the author's name (if it is given), the title of the article, the name of the newspaper, and the month, day, and year. If the city of the newspaper is not well known, include the state in parentheses. If the newspaper you are citing publishes more than one edition in a given day, cite the name of the edition in which the article appeared (for example, national edition, late edition). Page numbers are usually omitted, but ask your professor about his or her preference. If you are citing a large newspaper that is published in sections, include the name, letter, or number of the section.

N   29. Sarah Kaplan, "Part-human, part-pig embryo is grown in lab," *Washington Post*, January 27, 2017, sec. A.

An individual newspaper article is usually not listed in a bibliography unless it is of particular importance to your argument or you refer to it often. If you do list a newspaper article in your bibliography, use the following format.

B   Kaplan, Sarah. "Part-human, part-pig embryo is grown in lab." *Washington Post*, January 27, 2017, sec. A.

30. Online news source

Include the author, if known; the title of the article; the name of the newspaper or online service; the date of publication; and the URL.

N   30. "Afghan President's Brother, Ahmad Wali Karzai, Killed," *BBC News*, July 12, 2011, http://www.bbc.co.uk/news/world-middle-east-14118884.

B   "Afghan President's Brother, Ahmad Wali Karzai, Killed." *BBC News*, July 12, 2011. http://www.bbc.co.uk/news/world-middle-east-14118884.

31. Book review (print)

Begin with the reviewer's name, followed by the title of the review, if one is given. Follow this information by the words *review of*, the title of the work being reviewed, and its author. Also cite the periodical in which the review appears and the relevant publication information. If the author of the review is not named, begin with the title of the review or, if the review is untitled, with the words *Unsigned review of*.

N   31. Thomas J. Balcerski, review of *Regulating Passion: Sexuality and Patriarchal Rule in Massachusetts, 1700–1830*, by Kelly A. Ryan. *English Historical Review* 131 (2016): 1179.

B   Balcerski, Thomas J. Review of *Regulating Passion: Sexuality and Patriarchal Rule in Massachusetts, 1700–1830*, by Kelly A. Ryan. *English Historical Review* 131 (2016): 1179–1180.

Citation Guide
Articles in electronic databases

A typical citation for a journal article accessed from an electronic database includes the information below. See the next page for the corresponding note and bibliography entries, along with formatting tips.

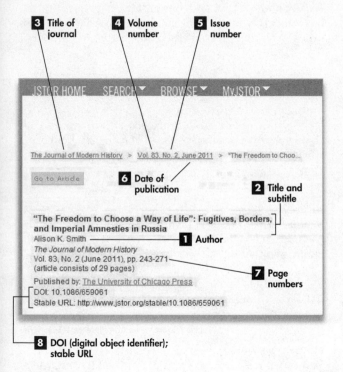

3 Title of journal

4 Volume number

5 Issue number

JSTOR HOME   SEARCH ▼   BROWSE ▼   MyJSTOR ▼

The Journal of Modern History > Vol. 83, No. 2, June 2011 > "The Freedom to Choo...

Go to Article

6 Date of publication

2 Title and subtitle

"The Freedom to Choose a Way of Life": Fugitives, Borders, and Imperial Amnesties in Russia
Alison K. Smith ——— **1** Author
The Journal of Modern History
Vol. 83, No. 2 (June 2011), pp. 243-271
(article consists of 29 pages)
Published by: The University of Chicago Press
DOI: 10.1086/659061
Stable URL: http://www.jstor.org/stable/10.1086/659061

7 Page numbers

8 DOI (digital object identifier); stable URL

Note

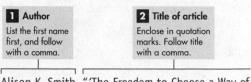

1. Alison K. Smith, "'The Freedom to Choose a Way of

Life': Fugitives, Borders, and Imperial Amnesties in Russia,"

Journal of Modern History 83, no. 2 (June 2011): 254,

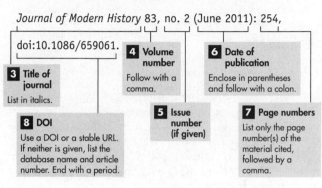

doi:10.1086/659061.

Bibliography

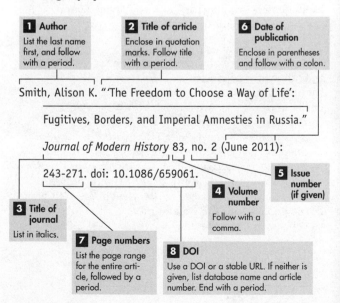

Smith, Alison K. "'The Freedom to Choose a Way of Life':

Fugitives, Borders, and Imperial Amnesties in Russia."

Journal of Modern History 83, no. 2 (June 2011):

243–271. doi: 10.1086/659061.

32. Online review

Include the name of the reviewer (if available), the title and author of the book being reviewed, the name of the online publication, the date of the review, the URL, and the date of access in parentheses if your instructor requires one or if no publication or modification date is given.

N   32. Unsigned review of *The True Flag: Theodore Roosevelt, Mark Twain, and the Birth of American Empire,* by Stephen Kinzer, *Kirkus Review,* October 11, 2016, https://www.kirkusreviews.com/book-reviews /stephen-kinzer/the-true-flag/.

B *Kirkus Review.* Unsigned review of *The True Flag: Theodore Roosevelt, Mark Twain, and the Birth of American Empire,* by Stephen Kinzer. October 11, 2016. https://www.kirkusreviews.com/book-reviews/stephen- kinzer/the-true-flag/.

Public documents (print and online)

For citing public documents such as presidential papers, legal cases, treaties, and constitutions, *Chicago* recommends the citation formats found in *The Bluebook: A Uniform System of Citation,* which is widely used by legal publications. In the United States, most federal government publications are made available in print and electronic forms. It is preferable to use print editions, but if you access a public document on-line, include the URL as the last element of the citation. The following models are for notes citing government documents commonly used by students writing history papers. Public documents are not typically cited in the bibliography.

33. Presidential papers

The public papers of most US presidents can be found in both print and electronic formats. Presidential papers including executive orders, speeches, press conferences, and so forth, are published in the *Public Papers of the Presidents of the United States* (Pub. Papers). They are also published in the *Weekly Compilation of Presidential Documents* (Weekly Comp. Pres. Doc.) and, from 2009, in the *Daily Compilation of Presidential Documents.* Your citation should include the title of the document; the volume number or issue number; the abbreviated name of the publication; the page number for the first page of the document; and the date on which the document was issued.

N   33. The President's News Conference on the Persian Gulf Crisis, 1 Pub. Papers 17 (January 9, 1991).

34. Supreme Court case

The decisions of the United States Supreme Court are published in *United States Reports* (U.S.). Your citation should begin with the case name, followed by the volume number, the abbreviated name of the publication, the number of the page on which the case begins, and the date of the decision.

N　　34. Roe v. Wade, 410 U.S. 113 (1973).

35. Treaty

Treaties signed prior to 1950 can be found in *United States Statutes at Large* (Stat.), which has been digitized by the Law Library of Congress. Treaties from 1950 or later can be found in either *United States Treaties and Other International Agreements* (U.S.T.) or *Treaties and Other International Acts Series* (T.I.A.S.). References to treaties should include the title of the treaty; the abbreviated names of the signatories (for bilateral agreements); a pinpoint reference, such as an article number, if appropriate; the date on which the treaty was signed; the abbreviated name of the treaty source (for example, U.S.T. or T.I.A.S.); the treaty or document number; and the page number, if relevant volume number and treaty number, as well as the publication year in parentheses; page numbers may be given.

N　　35. Mutual Defense Treaty Between the United States and the Republic of Korea; U.S.-Kor., art. 4, October 1, 1953, 5 U.S.T. 23602376.

36. Constitution

In a footnote or an endnote, the US Constitution and individual state constitutions are cited by the article (abbreviated *art.*) or amendment (*amend.*) number in roman numerals and the section (§) number in arabic numerals. References to the Constitution should not be included in your bibliography.

N　　36. U.S. Constitution, art. IV, § 1.

There are two Canadian Constitution Acts, The *Constitution Act, 1867* (formerly the *British North America Act, 1867*) and the *Constitution Act, 1982*. In a bibliography entry, they should be cited as follows:

B　　*Constitution Act, 1867* (UK), 30 & 31 Vict, c 3, reprinted in RSC 1985, App II, No 5.

B　　*Constitution Act, 1982*, being Schedule B to the *Canada Act of 1982* (UK), 1982, c.11.

If you want to refer to a particular section of these acts in a footnote, insert the section number immediately after the name of the document.

N   36. *Constitution Act, 1982*, s. 22, being Schedule B to the *Canada Act of 1982* (UK), 1982, c.11.

Multimedia sources

37. Film and video recordings

Begin with the title of the film or series, followed by the name of the director, publication information (including the original release, performance, or broadcast date, if appropriate, as well as the date of the recording's publication), and the medium (DVD, Blu-ray disc, VHS, etc.). If you are citing a particular episode in a series or a scene in a DVD, you can include the title, using the same format as you would for a chapter in a book.

N   37. *By the People: The Election of Barack Obama,* directed by Alicia Sams and Amy Rice, aired November 3, 2009 (New York: HBO Home Video, 2010), DVD.

B *By the People: The Election of Barack Obama.* Directed by Alicia Sams and Amy Rice. Aired November 3, 2009. New York: HBO Home Video, 2010. DVD, 116 minutes.

38. Published or broadcast interview

A citation for a published or broadcast interview should include the name of the person interviewed, the title of the interview (if any), the name of the person who conducted the interview, and the publication information for the source. If you have accessed the interview online, end your citation with the URL.

N   38. Joseph T. Glatthar, "General Lee's Army through Thick and Thin," interview by Peter S. Carmichael, *Civil War Times* 48, no. 1 (2009): 27.

B Glatthar, Joseph T., "General Lee's Army through Thick and Thin." Interview by Peter S. Carmichael. *Civil War Times* 48, no. 1 (2009): 26–27.

N   38. Mark Zuckerberg, interview by Lesley Stahl, *60 Minutes*, CBS, December 5, 2010, http://www.cbsnews.com/video/watch/?id =7120522n.

B Zuckerberg, Mark. Interview by Lesley Stahl. *60 Minutes*, CBS, December 5, 2010. http://www.cbsnews.com/video/watch/?id=7120522n.

For personal interviews, see model 45.

39. CD-ROM

Materials published on CD-ROM should be documented in the same way as printed works; indicate the medium at the end of the citation.

N   39. Dee Dyas, ed., *Pilgrims and Pilgrimage: Journey, Spirituality and Daily Life through the Centuries* (York, UK: University of York and St. John's College Nottingham, 2007), CD-ROM.

B   Dyas, Dee, ed. *Pilgrims and Pilgrimage: Journey, Spirituality and Daily Life through the Centuries*. York, UK: University of York and St. John's College Nottingham, 2007. CD-ROM.

40. Sound recording

Begin with the composer's name, followed by the title of the recording (italicized) and the name of the performer. Also provide the name of the recording company, the catalog number, and the date. For an anonymous work or a collection of works by several composers, begin with the title of the recording.

N   40. John Dowland, *The Queen's Galliard — Lute Music*, vol. 4, Nigel North, Naxos 8570284, 2009, compact disc.

B   Dowland, John. *The Queen's Galliard — Lute Music*. Vol. 4. Nigel North. Naxos 8570284, 2009, compact disc.

41. Sound or video recording accessed online

Provide the necessary information about the recording as listed in model 40. Also include any relevant descriptions about the original recording (such as the medium and the length), the website that is hosting the material, the digital format, and the URL. Include the access date if no date is provided or if your instructor requires it.

N   41. William Heise, *Annie Oakley* (Edison Manufacturing Co., 1894), 35 mm film, from Library of Congress, *Inventing Entertainment: The Motion Pictures and Sound Recordings of the Edison Companies*, MPEG video, 21 sec., http://memory.loc.gov/ammem/edhtml/edhome.html.

B   Heise, William. *Annie Oakley*. Edison Manufacturing Co., 1894, 35 mm film. From Library of Congress. *Inventing Entertainment: The Motion Pictures and Sound Recordings of the Edison Companies*. MPEG video, 21 sec. http://memory.loc.gov/ammem/edhtml/edhome.html.

N   41. Brittany Hughes, "A History of Istanbul," January 19, 2017, in History Extra, podcast, MP3 audio, http://www.historyextra.com/podcast/history-istanbul/.mp3.

B　Hughes, Brittany. "A History of Istanbul." History Extra, January 19, 2017. MP3 audio. http://www.historyextra.com/podcast/history -istanbul/.mp3

N　41. "What happened to global Chibok campaign?," produced by Marcus Thompson, BBC News, April 14, 2016, video, 2:26, https://www .youtube.com/watch?v=KlK-cypAWx4.

B　"What happened to global Chibok campaign?" Produced by Marcus Thompson. BBC News, April 14, 2016. Video, 2:26. https://www .youtube.com/watch?v=KlK-cypAWx4.

Unpublished sources

42. Thesis or dissertation
Include the author, title (in quotation marks), the kind of thesis, academic institution, and date. If you accessed the thesis online, include the URL after the date. If you accessed it through a database, include the name of the database and any identifying number in parentheses.

N　42. Tatiana Seijas, "Transpacific Servitude: The Asian Slaves of Mexico, 1580–1700" (PhD diss., Yale University, 2008), 67.

B　Seijas, Tatiana. "Transpacific Servitude: The Asian Slaves of Mexico, 1580–1700." PhD diss., Yale University, 2008.

43. Unpublished letter in a manuscript collection
Begin with the name of the letter writer, followed by the name of the recipient and the date. Follow with full identifying information about the collection in which the letter is found, beginning with the file, box, or container number, if known; the name of the collection; and its location.

N　43. Nathaniel Hawthorne to James W. Beekman, 9 April 1853, letter box 3, James W. Beekman Papers, New-York Historical Society, New York.

If you have cited only one item from a collection, your bibliography entry should list it according to the item's author.

B　Hawthorne, Nathaniel. Letter to James W. Beekman. James W. Beekman Papers. New-York Historical Society, New York.

44. Manuscript collection
If you have cited two or more items from a collection, the bibliography entry should cite the author and name of the collection, but not the specific items.

B　Beekman, James W. Papers. New-York Historical Society, New York.

45. Personal communications
Personal communications such as interviews, emails, telephone conversations, and so forth are usually cited in

a note, but are not listed in the bibliography. Your note should include the name of the person, information about the type of communication, and the date.

N   45. Jonathan Philips, telephone interview by author, August 4, 2014.

N   45. Tess Fletcher, email message to author, January 24, 2017.

Note: You should never include personal email addresses in your citations.

Internet and social media sources

For books and articles accessed online, you should follow the formats given in the models above. The following models provide instructions for how to cite original material that exists only on the World Wide Web, such as websites, blogs, and social media sites.

46. Web pages and websites

To cite a specific web page, include the title of the page; the title of the entire site; the name of the individual or group that owns or sponsors the site; the date of publication, modification, or revision, or, if none of these are available, the date you accessed the site; and the URL. Web pages are not usually cited in the bibliography, but important or frequently used websites or web pages may be included, listed under the owner or sponsor's name.

N   46. "Dread History: The African Diaspora, Ethiopianism, and Rastafari," *Migrations in History*, Smithsonian Institution, accessed October 6, 2014, http://www.smithsonianeducation.org/migrations/rasta /rasessay.html.

B   Smithsonian Institution. "Dread History: The African Diaspora, Ethiopianism, and Rastafari." *Migrations in History*. Accessed October 6, 2014. http://www.smithsonianeducation.org/migrations /rasta/rasessay.html.

47. Blog post

Include the author's name, the title of the entry (in quotation marks), the name of the blog (add the word *blog* in parentheses after the name if it does not use *blog*), the date of the post, and the URL. Blogs are not typically included in the bibliography. If a blog is important enough to be listed there, list it under the author's last name.

N   47. Lindsay Holst, "President Obama Speaks on Immigration Reform," *The White House Blog*, June 30, 2014, http://www.whitehouse .gov/blog/2014/06/30/president-obama-speaks-immigration-reform.

Citation Guide
Information from websites

A typical citation for original material found on a website includes as much of the information below as possible. See the next page for the corresponding note and bibliography entries, along with formatting tips.

3 Title of site

Famous Trials
by Douglas O. Linder (2011)
UNIVERSITY OF MISSOURI-KANSAS CITY (UMKC) SCHOOL OF LAW

Trial of Socrates (399 B.C.)

Gaius Verres Trial (70 B.C.)

Trial of Jesus (30 A.D.)

Martin Luther Trial (1521)

Salem Witchcraft Trials (1692)

John Peter Zenger Trial (1735)

"The Negro Plot" Trials (1741)

Boston Massacre Trials (1770)

5 URL
http://law2.umkc.edu/faculty/projects /ftrials/salem/SAL_ACCT.HTM

1 Author or sponsor of site

An account of the Salem witchcraft investigations, trials, and aftermath.

http://law2.umkc.edu/faculty/projects/ftrials/salem/SAL_ACCT.HTM

An account of the Salem witchcraft

The Witchcraft Trials in Salem: A Commentary
by Douglas Linder

2 Title of document or web page

O Christian Martyr Who for Truth could die
When all about thee Owned the hideous lie!
The world, redeemed from superstition's sway,
Is breathing freer for thy sake today.
--Words written by John Greenleaf Whittier and inscribed on a monument marking the grave of Rebecca Nurse, one of the condemned "witches" of Salem.

From June through September of 1692, nineteen men and women, all having been convicted of

Note

1 Title of document

Enclose in quotation marks. Follow title with a comma.

2 Title of site

Italicize only if the site is an online book or periodical. Follow with a comma.

3 Author or sponsor of site (if given)

List the first name first, and follow with a comma.

1. "The Witchcraft Trials in Salem: A Commentary,"

Famous Trials, Douglas Linder, accessed September 15, 2014,

http://law2.umkc.edu/faculty/projects/ftrials/salem

/SAL_ACCT.HTM.

5 URL

Follow with a period.

4 Access date

Include an access date if no publication date or modification date is given. Follow with a comma.

Bibliography

1 Author or sponsor of site (if given)

List the last name first, and follow with a period.

2 Title of document or web page

Enclose in quotation marks. Follow title with a period.

3 Title of site

Follow with a period.

Linder, Douglas. "The Witchcraft Trials in Salem: A

Commentary." Famous Trials. Accessed September 15,

2014. http://law2.umkc.edu/faculty/projects/ftrials

/salem/SAL_ACCT.HTM.

5 URL

Follow with a period.

4 Access date

Include an access date if no publication date or modification date is given. Follow with a period.

48. Social media

Many academic, research, and governmental institutions maintain social media pages. Notes should begin with the name of the person, group, or institution that authored the post, if known. Since social media posts do not have formal titles, include the text of the post up to 160 characters, in quotation marks. List the name of the social media platform (Facebook, Instagram, etc.) and the type of post (video, status update, etc.), if relevant; the date of the post; and the URL. Elements of the citation should be separated by commas. If you are citing a comment, include the name of the commentator, the content of the comment up to 160 characters, the date, and cite the original post (if you have already referred to the original post, you can shorten the reference). End with the URL.

N   48. The Library of Congress, "Today in History: Treaty of Paris is signed, formally ending Revolutionary War in America, 1783," Facebook status update, Sept. 3, 2017, https://www.facebook.com/NMAAHC /posts/10154691259431990.

N   48. NASA History Office (@NASAhistory), "#OTD in 1958, Pres. Eisenhower signed the National Aeronautics and Space Act - authorizing the creation of @NASA," Twitter, July 29, 2016, https://twitter.com /NASAhistory/status/759070995181371393.

N   48. Judith Wendell, "Ironic, isn't it, that people would have to rise in rebellion against slavery in a country founded on the 'self-evident' premise that all men are created equal," August 21, 2017, comment on Smithsonian National Museum of African American History and Culture, "On this date in 1831, enslaved people rose up against slaveholders in Southampton County, Virgina," https://www.facebook.com/NMAAHC /posts/10152904133676781?comment_id=012934857830112.

Citations to social media do not typically appear in the bibliography. If a social media source is used frequently or is otherwise important enough to include in your bibliography, use the following format.

B   The Library of Congress. "Today in History: Treaty of Paris is signed, formally ending Revolutionary War in America, 1783." Facebook status update, Sept. 3, 2017. https://www.facebook.com/NMAAHC /posts/10154691259431990.

7d Sample pages from a student research paper

Most of the suggestions in this book have been directed toward a single end: the production of a carefully researched, well-organized, and clearly written paper. On the following pages, you will find the title page, opening paragraphs, notes, and bibliography for one such paper.

Note: Some instructors prefer that you include information that would typically be found on the title page at the top of the first page of your paper. Always follow any guidelines your professor provides, or ask if you are not sure.

SAMPLE TITLE PAGE

1
TO TRY A MONARCH:
THE TRIALS AND EXECUTIONS OF CHARLES I OF ENGLAND
AND LOUIS XVI OF FRANCE

2 Lynn Chandler
3 History 362: Kings, Commoners, and Constitutions
4 Professor Geoffrey Roberts
5 November 22, 2014

1 Paper title, centered	**4** Instructor's name
2 Writer's name	**5** Date
3 Course title	

SAMPLE PAGE

Chandler 1

On January 30, 1649, Charles I, king of England, was beheaded.[1] The crowd around the scaffold greeted the sight of the severed head of their monarch with astonished silence. After lying in state for several days, the body was carried "in a Hearse covered with black Velvet, and drawn by six Horses, with four Coaches following it"[2] to Windsor Castle, where Charles was buried in royal estate beside Henry VIII and Queen Jane Seymour.[3] The scene was quite different on January 21, 1793, when another monarch ascended the scaffold--Louis XVI, king of France. In place of the silence that followed Charles's execution, Louis's decapitation was announced with a "flourish of trumpets" and the executioner's cry of "Thus dies a Traitor!"[4] Contemporaries reported that the crowd surged forward, dipped their handkerchiefs in the king's blood, and ran through the streets shouting "Behold the Blood of a Tyrant!"[5] The body was wrapped in canvas and brought in a cart to the Tuileries, where Louis XVI, the former king of France, was buried like a commoner.[6] These two events, separated by almost a century and a half, appear at first glance to be totally isolated from each other. A careful review of both official documents and private accounts, however, reveals that the chief actors in the drama surrounding the execution of Louis XVI were not only aware of the English precedent but referred to it again and again in the process of choosing their own courses of action, arguing for the validity of their point of view, and justifying their actions to the world.

The first clear-cut evidence that the French were influenced by the trial and execution of Charles I can be found in contemporary

---

1 Exact quotation appears in quotation marks; cited with endnote

2 Paraphrase cited with endnote

3 Writer's thesis

SAMPLE ENDNOTES PAGE

1   **2**

Notes

1. For a good general study of the execution, see Ann Hughes, "The Execution of Charles I," BBC, last modified February 17, 2011, http://www.bbc.co.uk/history/british/civil_war _revolution/charlesi_execution_01.shtml.

3

2. *England's Black Tribunal: The Tryal of King Charles the First* (printed for C. Revington, at the Bible and Crown in St. Paul's Churchyard, 1737), 55.

4

3. For a detailed account of the trial and execution of Charles I, see Graham Edwards, *The Last Days of Charles I* (Stroud, UK: Sutton, 1999). For a more recent biography, see Richard Cust, *Charles I* (Harlow, UK: Pearson Education, 2007).

5

4. Joseph Trapp, *The Trial of Louis XVI* (London, 1793), 205.

6

5. Trapp, *Trial,* 206.

6. Trapp, *Trial,* 145. For a detailed account of the trial and execution of Louis XVI, see David P. Jordan, *The King's Trial: The French Revolution vs. Louis XVI* (Berkeley: University of California Press, 1979).

7

7. Michael Walzer, ed., *Regicide and Revolution: Speeches at the Trial of Louis XVI*, trans. Marian Rothstein (Cambridge: Cambridge University Press, 1974), 1–89 passim.

8

8. Patricia Crawford, "'Charles Stuart, That Man of Blood,'" *Journal of British Studies* 16, no. 2 (1977): 53.

9

9. Keith Michael Baker, "French Political Thought at the Accession of Louis XVI," *Journal of Modern History* 50, no. 2 (1978): 283, http://www.jstor.org/stable/1877422.

10

10. Susan Dunn, *The Deaths of Louis XVI: Regicide and the French Political Imagination* (Princeton, NJ: Princeton University Press, 1994), 59.

11. Jordan, *King's Trial,* 122.

12. John Hardman, *The French Revolution Sourcebook* (London: Arnold, 1999), 178.

1 First line of note indented ½ inch

2 Full-size note number followed by a period

3 Note for a website

4 Discursive (or content) note

5 Note for a book

6 Author and title shortened in subsequent reference

7 Author's name listed in normal order (first name, last name)

8 Note for a journal article

9 Note for journal article accessed from a database

10 Notes are single-spaced; double-space between notes

SAMPLE BIBLIOGRAPHY

Bibliography

1 **2** Baker, Keith Michael. "French Political Thought at the Accession of Louis XVI." *Journal of Modern History* 50, no. 2 (1978): 279–303. http://www.jstor.org/stable/1877422.

3 Crawford, Patricia. "'Charles Stuart, That Man of Blood.'" *Journal of British Studies* 16, no. 2 (1977): 41–61.

4 Cust, Richard. *Charles I.* Harlow, UK: Pearson Education, 2007.

5 Dunn, Susan. *The Deaths of Louis XVI: Regicide and the French Political Imagination.* Princeton, NJ: Princeton University Press, 1994.

Edwards, Graham. *The Last Days of Charles I.* Stroud, UK: Sutton, 1999.

England's Black Tribunal: The Tryal of King Charles the First. Printed for C. Revington, at the Bible and Crown in St. Paul's Churchyard, 1737.

Hardman, John. *The French Revolution Sourcebook.* London: Arnold, 1999.

6 Hughes, Ann. "The Execution of Charles I." BBC. Last modified February 17, 2011. http://www.bbc.co.uk/history/state /monarchs_leaders/charlesi_execution_01.shtml.

Jennings, Jeremy. *Revolution and the Republic: A History of Political Thought in France since the Eighteenth-Century.* New York: Oxford University Press, 2011.

7 Jordan, David P. "In Defense of the King." *Stanford French Review* 1, no. 3 (1977): 325–38.

—. *The King's Trial: The French Revolution vs. Louis XVI.* Berkeley: University of California Press, 1979.

Trapp, Joseph. *The Trial of Louis XVI.* London, 1793.

Walzer, Michael, ed. *Regicide and Revolution: Speeches at the Trial of Louis XVI.* Translated by Marian Rothstein. Cambridge: Cambridge University Press, 1974.

1 First line of each entry at left margin; indent subsequent lines ½ inch

2 Bibliography entry for a journal article accessed from a database

3 Single-space entries; double-space between entries

4 List entries alphabetically by authors' last names

5 Bibliography entry for a book

6 Bibliography entry for a website

7 Bibliography entry for a journal article

Index